Seeing Women, Strengthening Democracy

Seeing Women, Strengthening Democracy

How Women in Politics Foster Connected Citizens

MAGDA HINOJOSA
AND
MIKI CAUL KITTILSON

OXFORD
UNIVERSITY PRESS

Oxford University Press is a department of the University of Oxford. It furthers
the University's objective of excellence in research, scholarship, and education
by publishing worldwide. Oxford is a registered trade mark of Oxford University
Press in the UK and certain other countries.

Published in the United States of America by Oxford University Press
198 Madison Avenue, New York, NY 10016, United States of America.

Library of Congress Cataloging-in-Publication Data
Names: Hinojosa, Magda, 1975– author. | Kittilson, Miki Caul, author.
Title: Seeing women, strengthening democracy : how women in politics foster connected
citizens / Magda Hinojosa and Miki Caul Kittilson.
Description: New York, NY : Oxford University press, 2020. | Includes bibliographical
references and index.
Identifiers: LCCN 2020012708 (print) | LCCN 2020012709 (ebook) |
ISBN 9780197526941 (hardback) | ISBN 9780197526965 (epub)
Subjects: LCSH: Women—Political activity—Latin America. | Women and democracy—Latin
America. | Women politicians—Latin America. | Women public officers—Latin America. |
Representative government and representation—Latin America. |
Latin America—Politics and government—21st century.
Classification: LCC HQ1236.5.L37 H559 2020 (print) | LCC HQ1236.5.L37 (ebook) |
DDC 320.082/098—dc23
LC record available at https://lccn.loc.gov/2020012708
LC ebook record available at https://lccn.loc.gov/2020012709

9 8 7 6 5 4 3 2

Printed by Integrated Books International, United States of America

CONTENTS

ACKNOWLEDGMENTS

This book would not have been possible without the generous support of the United States Agency for International Development (USAID). Funding from the USAID Democracy Fellows and Grants Program, Research and Innovation grant allowed us to conduct our panel surveys in Uruguay. We also could not have written this book without the Uruguayan women and men who generously shared their views as part of those surveys. We are also grateful to the political elites that granted interview requests. Their insights were invaluable to understanding the changes that we document in this book.

We would also like to thank the Latin American Public Opinion Project (LAPOP) and its major supporters (USAID, the Inter-American Development Bank, and Vanderbilt University) for making their data available, and especially wish to thank Rubí Arana for her assistance with data questions. Additionally, we would like to thank Maria Escobar-Lemmon and Michelle Taylor-Robinson for graciously sharing their data on women's representation in Latin American cabinets with us.

The early seeds of this project led us to organize a conference at Arizona State University on symbolic representation—and we are grateful to the School of Politics and Global Studies for funding that conference. We would like to thank all of the stellar conference participants for a discussion that shaped our ideas about representation and our conceptualization of the book. In particular, we thank Amanda Clayton, Mala Htun, and especially Leslie Schwindt-Bayer, for their helpful comments on our paper.

In addition to thanking the anonymous reviewers for their critical suggestions for revision, we also benefited from the advice of Jennifer Piscopo, Catherine Reyes-Housholder, and Gwynn Thomas. We are thankful to these scholars for reading chapters and providing helpful suggestions that ultimately allowed us to strengthen our contributions. Niki Johnson proved a tremendous resource; we appreciate her willingness to share her in-depth knowledge of Uruguay. We have also benefited greatly from having had the opportunity to present this work at meetings of the American Political Science Association. We are also grateful to have been able to present this work to enthusiastic audiences at Occidental College and Temple University, and thank Jennifer Piscopo and Hillel Soifer for those invitations.

For her support of this project and guidance through the publication process, we would like to thank Angela Chnapko, our editor at Oxford University Press. We are fortunate that our book is among the important works on women and politics published by Oxford University Press.

We would also like to thank several individuals at our home institution, Arizona State University. First and foremost, we would like to thank our friend, mentor, and colleague Kim Fridkin, who read and commented on chapters, provided valuable feedback on ideas, and co-authored our USAID Research and Innovation Grants working paper and our article in *Politics, Groups, and Identities*. Kim graciously agreed to work with us on the grant application that ultimately allowed us to carry out this research project. Although she only committed to stay on the project temporarily— because, as an Americanist, this work was quite far afield for her—and bowed out before beginning work on the book, we know that this book would not be what it is were it not for her.

We are grateful to Arizona State University president Michael Crow for funding to carry out fieldwork in Uruguay and to the School of Politics and Global Studies, which paid for a second round of fieldwork. The material gained from these interviews was critical to building our argument. We are also grateful to Patrick Kenney and Carolyn Warner for their insights on the book publishing process and to Rodney Hero for his thoughts on presenting our ideal case. The conversations that we had with Jennet Kirkpatrick about the concept of representation have enriched our work in fundamental ways. The careful research assistance of Alexandra Williams, Cristian Puga, and Pablo Ortega Poveda is greatly appreciated.

Even closer to home, we are thankful to our friends and families for their support. Miki would like to thank Greg, Michael, and Nikolas for their encouragement, support, and endless patience. In addition, Miki is particularly grateful to her mom, Shirley Caul, who has always been a powerful role model and visible symbol of doing meaningful work both within the family and in a career.

Magda would like to thank her husband, Daniel. Without his loving support she would have been unable to complete this book, and without his technical savvy, the maps presented in Chapter 1 would not exist. Roman (age 10) and Catalina (age 6) deserve special thanks for providing a much needed respite from work.

PROLOGUE

Laura Chinchilla recounts that while serving as President of Costa Rica, she would visit schools and—as we are all wont to do—would ask the children what they wanted to be when they grew up. One day, she asked one of the little boys, "Don't you want to be president when you grow up?"

The boy replied, "The thing is, you have to be a woman to be president."

—As told at the *Vital Voices* panel, Arizona State University, November 5, 2019

CHAPTER 1 | # Women and Politics Across Latin America

The impact [President Michelle Bachelet] had was symbolic, it's
cultural. It is very difficult to measure, but it's clear: suddenly little
girls know that it is possible to arrive there as women. And you will
find little girls that identify with her and they declare they want to be
presidents. This is a tremendous change in this country.

> —Teresa Valdés, Head of Gender Section, Chilean Ministry of Health
> (Jalalzai 2015: 189)

Now when a girl sees women on television, they are not just part of
fashion shows, they are exercising power, leading a country. They
start to see that it's possible that women will occupy those types of
positions.

> —Nielsen Pérez, Costa Rican Deputy (Cáceres 2018)

Like Teresa Valdés and Nielsen Pérez, many of us instinctively feel that
having women in office matters: that the election of Michelle Bachelet to
the presidency of Chile must have effects on those little girls watching
her on television. Indeed, little girls—and their mothers—can now turn
on their televisions or open up a newspaper and see women exercising
positions of political power.

Just a few years ago, more than 40 percent of Latin Americans were
governed by a female president, as Argentina, Brazil, Chile, and Costa
Rica simultaneously had women occupying the presidential palace. While
Cristina Fernández de Kirchner, Dilma Rousseff, Michelle Bachelet, and
Laura Chinchilla served in their nation's highest offices, many more women
have been competitive presidential candidates (such as Lourdes Flores and
Keiko Fujimori, both of Peru; Blanca Ovelar of Paraguay; Marina Silva of
Brazil; and Josefina Vásquez Mota in Mexico). While just 25 years ago,

Seeing Women, Strengthening Democracy. Magda Hinojosa and Miki Caul Kittilson, Oxford University Press (2020).
© Oxford University Press. DOI: 10.1093/oso/9780197526941.001.0001.

women held about 10 percent of legislative seats in the region, women now occupy more than a quarter of those positions. For instance, women now outnumber men in the Bolivian Chamber of Deputies. Sixty-five seats in the Mexican Senate belong to men, but 63 are held by women. In both Nicaragua and Costa Rica, women hold more than 45 percent of legislative seats. While these advances have not been felt uniformly across the countries of Latin America (women hold just 15 percent of seats in Brazil and Paraguay and only one of every eight seats in Guatemala's legislative assembly), these achievements are nonetheless impressive. Moreover, a number of Latin American countries have aimed to include more women in cabinets, and Bolivia, Chile, and Colombia have had parity cabinets. Moreover, this striking evolution in the gender makeup of Latin America's political elite is repeated at local levels, where more women than ever before occupy seats in municipal councils and as governors.

Little girls (and their mothers) have watched this evolution in political leadership, but because it is difficult to measure these symbolic effects, we know little about how women's increased numerical representation in politics affects citizens. Does the presence of more women in prominent elected positions affect how citizens connect with their political systems? Are male and female citizens equally affected?

The ways in which citizens connect to the democratic process are gendered, with women in many Latin American countries often expressing less political engagement than men. Dramatic increases in women's representation among political elites in most Latin American countries have not often been mirrored by gender equality at the mass level in terms of political interest, knowledge, efficacy, or political discussion. Women's inroads into formal political positions have not appeared to presage greater political engagement of this type. Beyond examining differing *levels* of political engagement and support among men and women, to fully understand how gender operates in processes of representation we must discern whether different drivers affect men's and women's connections to democracy. Based on the historic exclusion of women from the political arena in most political systems around the world, men and women may view elections and political events through distinct lenses.

Given the commitment to increasing the numbers of women in office worldwide—with more than 70 countries across the globe legislating affirmative action measures to boost women's representation in politics—we endeavor to know more about how women's increasing presence among political elites matters for gender differences in political engagement and political support. We contend that when and where women's numbers rise substantially in national legislatures, female citizens feel more connected to the political process and consequently pay more attention to political happenings and perceive themselves as more capable of making sense of the political process. As citizens see that "people like me" have a voice in congress, this leads to changes in how they interact with government and through the political process.

This inclusion benefits democracy in a number of ways. As part of a set of democratic principles, inclusion goes hand in hand with equality and fairness. While significant attention is given to equality in voting participation, it is equally important for robust democracies to examine citizens' active engagement with and attitudes toward the democratic process and the development of their individual political capacities (Warren 2002). Diverse perspectives, often rooted in different lived experiences, expand and enrich collective deliberations. By contrast, systematic disaffection muffles voices, lowering the quality of those deliberations. In Dahl's well-known criteria for democracy, these principles are enshrined as equal and effective participation in disseminating points of view and shaping the political agenda (1971; 1982).

Women's Increased Presence in Latin American Politics

Headlines scream out: "Historic number of women in Congress" and "For the first time, there's gender equality in the composition of the candidate lists" (OEM Editors 7/11/2018; Fitz Patrick 2019). There are now more women in politics in Latin America than ever before. Names like Michelle Bachelet and Cristina Fernández de Kirchner are recognized around the globe.

But, these two women are far from alone in having scaled the highest political peaks. Since 1990, women have been elected to their nation's highest office nine times in Latin America. Both Argentina and Chile not only elected women presidents but re-elected these women as well. As Table 1.1 shows, viable female presidential candidates have been a reality in 12 of the 18 Latin American countries.[1] Moreover, Argentina (2007), Brazil (2014), and Chile (2013) have had presidential elections featuring more than one competitive female candidate.

---

[1] We follow conventions in the study of Latin American politics and consider only the Spanish-speaking countries and Brazil to constitute Latin America. We also exclude Cuba from any of our analyses given the lack of any reliable survey data for the country and the fact that it has been consistently authoritarian.

TABLE I.I Women's Representation as Viable Presidential Candidates in Latin America

YEAR	COUNTRY	CANDIDATE	% VOTE	ELECTED
1990	Nicaragua	Violeta Chamorro	55	✓
1997	Honduras	Nora de Melgar	43	✗
1998	Colombia	Noemi Sanín	27	✗
1999	Panama	Mireya Moscoso	30	✓
2001	Peru	Lourdes Flores	24	✗
2005	Chile	Michelle Bachelet	46	✓
2006	Peru	Lourdes Flores	24	✗
2007	Argentina	Cristina Fernández de Kirchner	45	✓
2007	Argentina	Elisa Carrió	23	✗
2008	Paraguay	Blanca Olevar	32	✗
2009	Panama	Balbina Herrera	38	✗
2010	Costa Rica	Laura Chinchilla	47	✓
2010	Brazil	Dilma Rousseff	42	✓
2011	Argentina	Cristina Fernández de Kirchner	54	✓
2011	Peru	Keiko Fujimori	21	✗
2012	Mexico	Josefina Vázquez	26	✗
2013	Honduras	Xiomara Castro de Zelaya	29	✗
2013	Chile	Evelyn Matthei	25	✗
2013	Chile	Michelle Bachelet	47	✓
2014	Brazil	Marina Silva	21	✗
2014	Brazil	Dilma Rousseff	41	✓
2015	Guatemala	Sandra Torres	20	✗
2016	Peru	Keiko Fujimori	40	✗
2017	Chile	Beatriz Sánchez	20	✗
2019	Guatemala	Sandra Torres	26	✗

NOTE: The percentage of the vote refers only to the percentage obtained in the first and/or only round of voting. The information provided includes only those presidential candidates considered viable. Using the definition utilized by Reyes-Housholder and Thomas 2019, candidates are considered viable if they obtained a minimum of 20 percent of the vote.

SOURCE: Reyes-Housholder and Thomas 2019; supplemental data on Sandra Torres obtained from Guatemala's Supreme Electoral Tribunal 2019.

Women are also now better represented in cabinet ministries. Although ministers in presidential cabinets in Latin America are appointed and not elected, they still hold enormous policymaking power, making their entrance into the executive branch an important component in surveying women's rising power among those who govern (Escobar-Lemmon and Taylor-Robinson 2016).

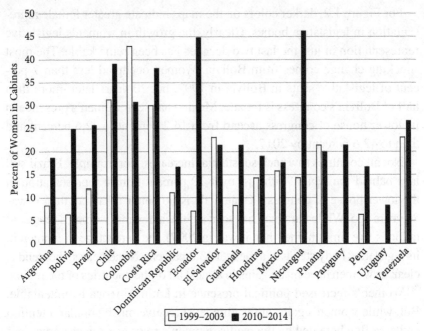

FIGURE 1.1 Women's Representation in Latin America's Cabinets

NOTE: Data indicates the percentage of women in the president's initial cabinets for the time periods 1999–2003 and 2010–2014.

SOURCE: Escobar-Lemmon and Taylor-Robinson 2016; Taylor-Robinson 2018.

The data in Figure 1.1 on women's representation in presidential cabinets in Latin America indicate a general upward trend. Women are more politically present in 2010–2014 than they were in these cabinet positions in 1999–2003. On average, women held only 15.3 percent of ministerial positions in the earlier time period, but slightly over a quarter of these in the latter time period.[2] Notably, women held no cabinet positions in Paraguay or Uruguay in the first time period, but in the time period from 2010–2014, all incoming presidents included some female representation in their cabinets. The percentage of women in Brazil's cabinet doubled, rising from about 12 percent to just over 25 percent. Only Colombia, El Salvador, and Panama reversed course, marking a decrease in women's representation in cabinets over this period of time. Selecting parity cabinets has been a point of pride for presidents Michelle Bachelet of Chile and Evo Morales of Bolivia, among others.

---

[2] Given the small numbers of cabinet members (often around 20), even replacing one woman with a man can change the percentage of female ministers appreciably.

For Figure 1.2, darker colors on the maps indicate greater female representation in legislative bodies. Clearly, the growth in women's legislative representation in just the last two decades has been remarkable. The most shocking change comes from Bolivia. Women occupied less than 7 percent of legislative seats in Bolivia in 1997, but 20 years later, more than half of Bolivia's congress is female. Mexico has seen women's presence in its lower house of congress ascend from 14.2 percent to 22.6 percent and then to 42.6 percent by 2017.

Not all countries saw such substantial increases. For example, Brazil still lags behind the region with just over 10 percent female representation in the lower house of congress. Guatemala is no better off today than it was 20 years ago. While Paraguay has seen significant gains (women's representation is five times higher than it was in 2007), the percentage of women in its legislative body stands at a meager 13.8 percent. Nonetheless, the trend is clear, as women have made gains in almost all of the countries of the region.

Women's increased political presence in Latin America is undeniable. But, while women's gains at the elite level receive much popular attention and are often heralded by the media, women's roles as citizens garner less attention, and the connection between the two even less (Kittilson 2016). Yet, the political connectedness of female citizens is vital to democracy.

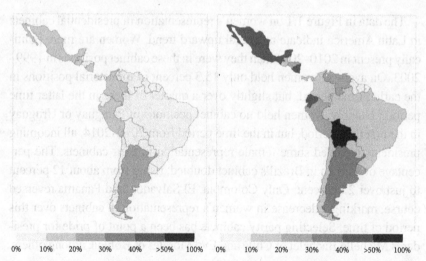

0% 10% 20% 30% 40% >50% 100%   0% 10% 20% 30% 40% >50% 100%

FIGURE 1.2 Women's Representation in Latin America's Legislatures, 1997 & 2017

NOTE: Data for 1997 is from January 1. Data was unavailable for Ecuador for that date; the Ecuadorian data comes from the next available date in 1997: November 10. All 2017 data is from January 1. All data presented is for lower houses or unicameral bodies.

SOURCE: IPU 2019.

In the sections that follow, we examine both political engagement and political support variables to better understand what strengthens the connections between (male and female) citizens and the political process.

Political Connectedness: Key to Democracy

A rich literature has emerged on inequalities in political participation, focusing mainly on activities such as voting, contributing to a political campaign, canvassing for a candidate, or taking part in a political march. Yet, less scholarly attention is given to understanding gender differences in orientations toward the democratic process. In this book, we examine a wide array of political orientations and attitudes, focusing on how changes in the political context differentially affect men's and women's ties to democratic institutions and processes.

First, we delve into political engagement, which encompasses a set of "psychological orientations toward politics" that citizens hold (Burns, Schlozman, and Verba 2001: 335). These orientations are an integral component of individuals' connections to the democratic process. In their classic book setting out the civic voluntarism model, Verba, Schlozman, and Brady discuss the importance of psychological predispositions and orientations such as political interest, efficacy, and knowledge, which can pull citizens into the democratic process (1995: 272, 344).

An informed, knowledgeable, and confident citizenry is essential to a strong democracy. At the individual level, political engagement signals the orientations and skills that are essential to full democratic citizenship (Mansbridge 1980). In addition, political engagement fosters political activity among men and women alike (Burns, Schlozman, and Verba 2001). Thus, less politically engaged citizens may participate in politics less, or in different ways from those who are more cognitively engaged in the political arena. In the aggregate, robust levels of political engagement contribute to representation and equality in the democratic process. Citizens who are interested in, feel efficacious and knowledgeable about, and discuss politics can shape the issue and policy agendas and inform public opinion. We therefore examine political knowledge, political interest, political discussion, and political efficacy in this book.

Although the dimensions of political engagement are distinct, they are also linked in complex and reinforcing ways. Political knowledge is often seen as a prerequisite for other forms of political engagement (Verba, Schlozman, and Brady 1995). Knowledge about politics helps citizens form coherent policy positions and may even spark further attention to political matters. Political interest motivates individuals to become politically active and can also encourage the acquisition of political information, cognitive processing, discussing, and even efficacious attitudes toward navigating the political process. Political efficacy can be external or internal, tapping into individuals' feelings about whether they are able to effectively understand political processes and whether their actions make a difference for government outputs.

Both political interest and efficacy make it more likely that citizens will join political conversations in their everyday lives. Certainly political discussion can be categorized as an activity (following Verba, Burns, and Schlozman 1997: 1056), but we will consider it as part of this set of orientations that indicate engagement. Importantly, routine political discussion is not aimed at influencing elected officials, but rather seeks to communicate interests and positions, exchange information, and potentially influence peers. Political discussion is essential to raising the salience of particular issues and to shaping the alternatives and potential solutions to societal issues.

Second, we examine political support. While political engagement is the backbone of a well-functioning democracy, trust and satisfaction with government and the political system affect citizens' political behavior and their attitudes (Almond and Verba 1963). Positive feelings toward democratic institutions underpin healthy connections to the democratic process, and citizens who lack faith in government and its institutions are unlikely to participate politically or to respect political outcomes.

The sentiments that citizens display toward the political system are evident in their confidence in and approval of the regime and its institutions (Easton 1965). Trust, confidence, and satisfaction with the regime are vital to the quality of democratic representation and to the stability of the regime itself. Understanding how and why political support varies can help us to understand the ties that connect citizens to their government. Although most previous research assumes the determinants of political support are uniform, we suggest that political change affects men's and women's levels of support in different ways.

Blais, Morin-Chassé, and Singh cogently remind us that "perceptions of the extent to which democracy performs its representational function are known to affect behavior and attitudes in the public" (2017: 232). We explore several different measures of citizens' views of the representative process and its institutions. Specifically, we test how visible and sizable gains in women's officeholding affect mass-level political support, including trust in elections, confidence in democratic institutions, pride in the way the political system works, and satisfaction with democracy more broadly.

Why are gender inequalities in political connections troubling for the vitality of democracy? While overall levels of political engagement and support are important to the strength of the democratic process, so too are potential inequalities in these among politically relevant groups (Lijphart 1997; Verba, Schlozman, and Brady 1995). If disengagement or lack of support are randomly distributed, this may be less problematic for the democratic process. However, if disengagement is systematic and particular groups are underrepresented in their interest, discussion, or confidence in navigating politics, then the causes of this inequality are less likely to reside with the individual and instead are likely shaped by the political system, its processes, and its policies. Similarly, if some citizens are more politically supportive than others, and these differences are clustered differently among politically relevant groups, then we can also assume that these inequities are a function of the political system.

Beyond inequalities in outcome, to fully understand why and how citizens connect to politics we must consider the different drivers for traditionally underrepresented groups. Due to the traditionally gendered division of labor in society and the economy, women may bring different experiences, perspectives, or policy preferences to their engagement and interaction with politics and to their support for government. Taken together, we use political engagement and political support as our indicators of citizens' connections and commitments to the democratic process.

Political Connectedness in Latin America

In recent years, the news media have repeatedly issued warnings of a crisis of representation in Latin America. Reports often claim that citizens are dissatisfied with democracy, disenchanted with political parties, and distrustful of political institutions. Profound discontent with the political system may produce widespread citizen apathy, invite the rise of political outsiders, and generate the collapse of party systems. This brewing dissatisfaction may be "eroding support for democracy" (Levitsky 2018: 103). Such exhortations have put democracies on high alert.

Low levels of political engagement and political support in Latin America are often startling—although, as contemporary headlines trumpet, Latin America is hardly alone in facing such a crisis of representation. Importantly, levels of political engagement and support are far from uniform in countries across the region. Latin American countries differ in important ways in their legacies of political engagement, political support, and political participation. Historical circumstances and political events—including long experiences of authoritarianism—have altered psychological orientations and shaped how citizens engage with politics, trust their governments, and evaluate their democratic experiences (Carlin, Singer, and Zechmeister 2015). Below, we use data on political interest and satisfaction with democracy to exemplify the substantial differences in political engagement and political support that exist across the Latin American region.

The Latin American Public Opinion Project (LAPOP) surveys allow us to observe some of these cross-national differences. Because the timing of the LAPOP surveys in relation to national elections differs considerably, for each figure in this chapter we include all waves in the 2004–2019 merged dataset. By drawing together the surveys, we hope to smooth some of the inherent differences in political interest that may naturally wax and wane with approaching election campaigns.

We see significant variation in political interest across Latin America. Figure 1.3 shows the total percentage of respondents (both men and

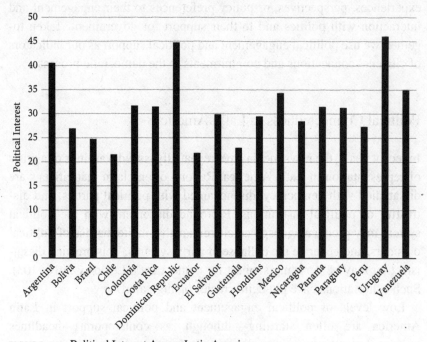

FIGURE 1.3 Political Interest Across Latin America
SOURCE: LAPOP 2004–2019 Merged Dataset.

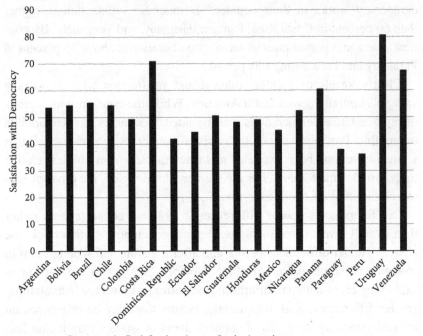

FIGURE 1.4 Democratic Satisfaction Across Latin America
SOURCE: LAPOP 2004–2019 Merged Dataset.

women) in a country who report having "some" or "a lot" of interest in politics.[3] In the Dominican Republic, for example, nearly 45 percent report at least some political interest. Similarly, 40 percent of the Argentine public reports high levels. By contrast, in Chile and Ecuador only approximately 22 percent of respondents report at least some political interest. Political interest in the Dominican Republic is twice as high as it is in Ecuador.

Figure 1.4 displays the total percentage of respondents (both men and women) who report being "somewhat" or "very satisfied" with the way

---

[3] This graph includes data for all countries in which this question was asked between 2004–2019: Argentina (2008), Bolivia (2004, 2006, 2008), Brazil (2007, 2008, 2010, 2012, 2014), Chile (2006, 2008), Colombia (2004, 2006, 2008, 2010, 2012, 2014, 2018), Costa Rica (2004, 2006, 2008, 2010, 2012, and 2014), Dominican Republic (2004, 2006, 2008, 2010, 2012, 2014, 2016, 2019), Ecuador (2004, 2006, 2008, 2010, 2012, 2016), El Salvador (2004, 2006, 2008, 2010, 2012, 2014, 2016, 2018), Guatemala (2004, 2006, 2008, 2010, 2012, 2014, 2017, 2019), Honduras (2004, 2006, 2008, 2010, 2012, 2014, 2016, 2018), Mexico (2004, 2006, 2008, 2010, 2012, 2014, 2016, 2019), Nicaragua (2004, 2006, 2008, 2010, 2012, 2014, 2016, 2019); Panama (2004, 2006, 2008, 2010, 2012, 2014), Paraguay (2006, 2008, 2010, 2012, 2014, 2016, 2019), Peru (2006, 2008, 2010, 2012, 2014, 2017, 2019), Uruguay (2007, 2008, 2010, 2012, 2014), and Venezuela (2007, 2008).

democracy works in their country.[4] Democratic satisfaction is higher than 60 percent in Costa Rica, Panama, Uruguay, and Venezuela. By contrast, average reported rates of satisfaction barely rise above 35 percent in Paraguay and Peru during this period.

Clearly, levels of political interest and satisfaction with democracy vary substantially across Latin America. While the concern with a crisis of representative democracy is well-founded, it assumes the electorate is monolithic. Previous work on the crisis of democracy ignores the fact that women have long been excluded and disconnected from politics relative to their male counterparts. For the women of the region, the crisis of representation may be "politics as usual."

Our focus is on gender differences in political connectedness rather than overall levels of political engagement or support. In this book, we analyze gender differences before and after a visible and sizable jump in women's presence in elected office. Notably, factors that may go far in explaining cross-national differences may offer less leverage in explaining gender differences. And, importantly, factors that may be consequential for understanding the political connectedness of women may matter less for explaining men's political connections.

Gender Differences in Political Connectedness: Still Puzzling

Today, gender differences in voter turnout are minimal in many democracies (Pintor and Gratschew 2002; Norris 2002; Conway 2001; Christy 1987; Inglehart and Norris 2003; Coffé and Bolzendahl 2010). In cross-national analysis, Norris 2002 concludes that "any tendency for women to vote less frequently than men in the past seems to have disappeared in established democracies" (101), although some differences persist in newer democracies. Across Latin America, there are few statistically significant

---

[4] The dataset includes this question for Argentina (2008), Bolivia (2004, 2006, 2008), Brazil (2007, 2008, 2010, 2012, 2014), Chile (2006. 2008), Colombia (2004, 2006, 2008, 2010, 2012, 2014, 2018), Costa Rica (2004, 2006, 2008, 2010, 2012, 2014), Dominican Republic (2004, 2006, 2008, 2010, 2012, 2014, 2016, 2019), Ecuador (2004, 2006, 2008, 2010, 2012, 2016), El Salvador (2004, 2006, 2008, 2010, 2012, 2014, 2016, 2018), Guatemala (2004, 2006, 2008, 2010, 2012, 2014, 2017, 2019), Honduras (2004, 2006, 2008, 2010, 2012, 2014, 2016, 2018), Mexico (2004, 2006, 2008, 2010, 2012, 2014, 2016, 2019), Nicaragua (2004, 2006, 2008, 2010, 2012, 2014, 2016, 2019), Panama (2004, 2006, 2008, 2010, 2012, 2014), Paraguay (2006, 2008, 2010, 2012, 2014, 2016, 2019), Peru (2006, 2008, 2010, 2012, 2014, 2017, 2019), Uruguay (2007, 2008, 2010, 2012, 2014), and Venezuela (2007, 2008).

differences between men and women in voter participation (Espinal and Zhao 2015; Azpuru 2017).

Beyond voting, gender gaps in other forms of participation have persisted. Looking at 18 industrialized democracies, scholars found that men are more likely to participate in protests, contact politicians, join parties, and attend political meetings (Coffé and Bolzendahl 2010). Kittilson and Schwindt-Bayer 2010 found that in the democracies included in the Comparative Study of Electoral Systems project, men are more likely than women to contact public officials and volunteer on political campaigns. In an analysis of Latin America, gender gaps in less traditional forms of political participation (which included taking part in demonstrations, blocking traffic, or participating in occupations) remained statistically significant in all countries except Guatemala and Costa Rica (Desposato and Norrander 2009). And these patterns across Latin America continue in more recent years, with women less likely to protest or work for a political party (Espinal and Zhao 2015).

Gender gaps in political engagement remain even more common than these gaps in political participation. Across democracies, men routinely score higher on assessments of political knowledge (Burns, Schlozman, and Verba 2001; Kittilson 2018; Fraile and Gomez 2017a). Dassonneville and McAllister 2018 analyze 106 election years across a variety of democracies and find that, in all but one, men show higher levels of political knowledge. And these gender gaps in knowledge persist in recent years.

Analyzing 31 democracies in the Comparative Study of Electoral Systems project, Kittilson and Schwindt-Bayer 2010 found that men remain more politically interested and knowledgeable than women, more likely to discuss politics, and more likely to attempt to politically persuade others. And these gender differences are typically statistically significant. Specific to political discussion, Nir and McClurg (2015) find that men report higher levels of conversation across 33 countries. Similarly, gender differences in engagement have been well documented for the United States and Britain (Verba, Burns, and Schlozman 1997).

Examining just Latin America, Desposato and Norrander 2009 found similar patterns: men are more likely than women to follow political news, to have political discussions, and to persuade others politically; the gender gaps in these forms of political engagement are statistically significant in all countries of the region except Costa Rica. Similarly, across Latin America even into 2012, women are less likely to report political interest, and among women those younger and with less education are even less interested (Azpuru 2017).

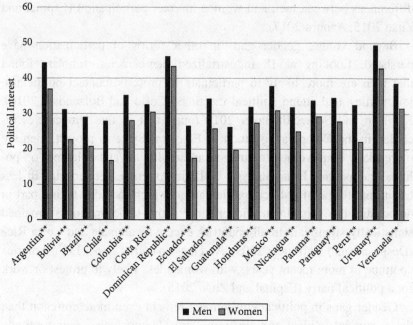

FIGURE 1.5 Gender Gaps in Political Interest Across Latin America

NOTE: Percentage reporting a lot or some political interest. ***p<.001; **p<.01; *p<.05.

SOURCE: LAPOP 2004–2019 Merged Dataset.

These gender gaps in engagement appear firmly entrenched in Latin America. Drawn from the LAPOP survey data, Figure 1.5 displays gender gaps in reported political interest in Latin America by country.[5] The pattern is unmistakable: in all countries, men report being more politically interested than women. Importantly, the gender gap in political interest exceeds seven percentage points in half of the countries (Argentina, Bolivia, Brazil, Chile, Colombia, Ecuador, El Salvador, Peru, and Venezuela). In all countries, the differences in political interest reported by men and women are statistically significant.

Confidence in one's own ability to understand the most important political issues is part of a citizen's engagement with the democratic process. The self-confidence to navigate the political landscape taps the concept of internal political efficacy and is an integral component of being a connected democratic citizen. Gender differences in political efficacy are

---

[5] Please refer to footnote 3 for information on the countries and years in which this question appears in the merged dataset.

less likely to stem from differential resources than from contextual cues that either signal women are capable and accepted in the political sphere or are not.

We therefore also examine the average scores for men and for women on their self-reported understanding of important issues in 2014 (the corresponding figure appears in the online appendix, available at: http:// www.public.asu.edu/~mhinojo1/books.html). Respondents rate their understanding on a scale from 1 to 7, with 1 signifying strong disagreement and 7 the strongest agreement. For every country in which this question was asked in the LAPOP survey, the differences between men and women are statistically significant. The magnitude of the gap is larger than half a point (on the 7-point scale) in half of the countries and greater than .20 in the remainder. The largest differences between men and women are in Colombia. Men average 4.2 and women average 3.3, and the differences between them are statistically significant.

Political discussion is another integral dimension of political engagement. Discussing political topics is a behavior, but not one necessarily aimed directly at political authorities. Instead, discussion among citizens shapes attitudes, builds connections among citizens, and influences their orientations toward elections, policies, officeholders, and institutions. Importantly, the effects of political discussion are to shape the broader political discourse and agenda. In this way, political discussion (or its absence) taps into how citizens connect to the democratic process in their daily life.

We document strikingly large gender differences in political discussion across Latin America in 2008. The survey data reports the percentages of men and women who say that they discuss politics a few times per month or more. The gaps measure more than 7 percentage points in all countries listed except Honduras. Further, these differences are statistically significant in each case. Peru yields one of the largest gender gaps, where men are nearly twice as likely as women to report discussing politics frequently. Among men, nearly 41 percent discuss politics frequently while among women, 21 percent report the same. The percentage-point difference between men and women is nearly 20 in Argentina and Bolivia, and 15 percentage points in Chile. Mexico also registers a large gender gap with nearly 43 percent of men reporting they discuss politics frequently while only 26 percent of women report the same. Nicaragua, Honduras, and Costa Rica all yield some of the smallest gender differences in frequency of political discussion. The online appendix includes a graph with this information.

A more limited number of studies explore gender differences in political support, and nearly all of this research has focused on emerging democracies in Central and Eastern Europe in the 1990s. Among those studies, there is little consensus about how gender structures political support. On the one hand, some studies find higher levels of political support among women. For example, Johnson 2005 finds women are more trusting of political institutions in Poland and Ukraine. On the other hand, several studies find men more supportive of their democratic system. When it comes to support for democratic norms and values and democratic performance in Eastern and Central Europe and Russia, women appeared less supportive in the 1990s (Gibson, Duch, and Tedin 1992; Oakes 2002; Waldron-Moore 1999). In one of the few studies comparing gender differences in democratic values across Latin America, Azpuru 2017 finds women less likely to support democracy than their male counterparts. Similarly, Arana and Santacruz Giralt 2005 find that Salvadoran women express less trust than men in key political institutions.

Drawing on the LAPOP data, Figure 1.6 displays levels of democratic satisfaction for men and for women across Latin America.[6] Here, we see fewer gender differences, although differences between men and women in democratic satisfaction are statistically significant in Bolivia, Brazil, Colombia, the Dominican Republic, Ecuador, Paraguay, Peru, and Uruguay. It is important to consider whether inclusion at the elite level leads to changes in men's and women's levels of political support.

Both political engagement and support encompass a variety of dimensions, and we have presented several measures of these concepts here. By including several measures, we seek to uncover patterns in men's and women's relationships with the political processes of their countries. Taken together, these cross-national data demonstrate that gender gaps in political engagement still endure and are statistically significant. Further, these gender gaps in political engagement are not only commonplace, they also persist alongside gains such as the election of female presidents, the presidential candidacies of women, and even the passage and strengthening of women-friendly legislation. The cross-national results presented in Figure 1.6 suggest that there are fewer gender differences in political support, yet we must better understand whether changes in the composition of elected officials differentially affect men and women.

[6] Please refer to footnote 4 for information on the countries and years in which this question appears in the merged dataset.

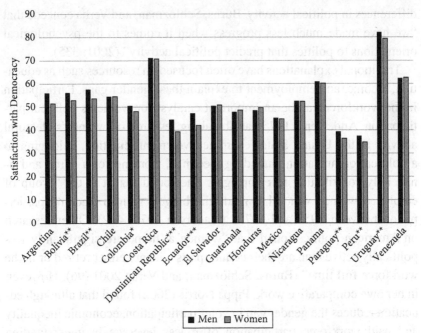

FIGURE 1.6 Gender Gaps in Democratic Satisfaction Across Latin America

NOTE: Percentage reporting that they are satisfied or very satisfied with the way democracy works in their country. ***p<.001; **p<.01; *p<.05.

SOURCE: LAPOP 2004–2019 Merged Dataset.

Recent comparative research on democratic participation and attitudes emphasizes the importance of contextual influences across a variety of regions including Latin America (Carlin, Singer, and Zechmeister 2015; Booth and Seligson 2009; Dalton and Anderson 2011). Across Latin America, some of the most important contextual factors include the more fluid party system, electoral volatility, emergence of outsider politicians, legacy of economic crises in the 1980s and 1990s, and importance of accountability voting (Carlin, Singer, and Zechmeister 2015). However, the bulk of this research often pays less attention to the differential effects of contextual factors for men and women. In particular, the rise of "outsiders" in the political arena has most recently included a group long excluded from positions of power: women.

Previous Explanations for Gender Differences in Political Attitudes

Persistent gender gaps in political orientations have puzzled scholars of political behavior for decades. In their groundbreaking book on gender differences in political activity, Burns, Schlozman, and Verba concede that "we have made much less progress when it comes to the psychological orientations to politics that predict political activity" (2001: 335).

Traditional explanations have often focused on resources such as education, income, and employment to explain these gender gaps. Participation in the workforce can be an important catalyst for women's political participation. Andersen's 1975 path-breaking research on women's electoral activity in the United States examined voter participation, belonging to a political organization, attending meetings, working for a party, and financially contributing to campaigns. She found that it is the "group of employed women which has made the biggest gain in electoral participation between 1952 and 1972" (Andersen 1975: 442). Other research on American politics found that "women at home are significantly less politically active than are their counterparts who are either retired or in the workforce full time" (Burns, Schlozman, and Verba 2001: 96). However, in her own comparative work, Pippa Norris (2002) found that although education reduces the gender gap in voter participation, economic inequality and paid workforce participation offer less leverage in understanding these gaps.

Moreover, women's workforce participation can have a deleterious effect on women's political participation. While employment outside the home may improve income and civic skills, it can also limit the amount of free time an individual has for civic activities. In his influential work on social capital, Robert Putnam (2000) linked declining community involvement in the late 1900s to women's entrance into the paid labor force. Furthermore, Schlozman, Burns, and Verba 1999 found that women reap fewer skills and resources from labor force participation, in part because they are less likely to gain access to the same high-level jobs as men. In other words, gains in education and employment levels do not necessarily lead to gender egalitarian occupational status and income levels. Women's work is routinely marginalized in sectors that are undervalued and underpaid. Iversen and Rosenbluth 2006 highlighted the trajectories of women's paid employment and the public sector.

However, factors such as these have exerted less influence than commonly expected over political engagement and attitudes. Conventional resource-based explanations had suggested that as women's educational levels rose, as their participation in the workforce increased, and as their incomes grew, gender gaps in political engagement would disappear. Yet this has not automatically been the case. Importantly, gender differences in political engagement have endured despite broad-based societal changes.

Scholars also turned to the role of culture and political socialization to explain why these gender gaps in political engagement persist. Traditional gender roles may limit women's access to the public sphere, thereby decreasing political engagement among women, whereas the spread of more egalitarian gender roles may encourage women to become more politically connected. Specifically, attitudes that limit women's place in society to the private sphere may also curb women's proclivity to pay attention to politics or feel a sense of trust in the political process and its institutions. Inglehart and Norris's 2003 influential book draws on cross-national survey data to demonstrate the effects of economic development and religious traditions on attitudes toward gender equality in politics. They find that more egalitarian views of gender roles lessen the differences between men and women in political participation.

Political context can condition these processes of socialization. Contextual influences can either draw women into the political process or push them away. Explanations that prioritize contextual influences diverge from individual resources or socialization explanations. Burns 2007 theorizes that the salience of particular issues or policies can play an integral role in engaging women in the political process. By extension, women may be more or less likely to mobilize depending upon the perceived relevance of particular issues. For example, in the midst of a significant event that focuses national attention on domestic violence, we would expect that political context would drive more women to become politically engaged.

Aggregate levels of women's rising education and workforce participation and more egalitarian attitudes toward women's roles in the political arena certainly contribute to ameliorating gender gaps in political engagement over time. These changes, however, are rarely speedy. In addition to these incremental social processes, we build upon previous research to emphasize the importance of political context, in part because here we see that change can come overnight.

Only a handful of past studies offer potential explanations for gender differences in political support, and some differing explanatory factors appear to work in opposing ways. Research in newer democracies often finds lower levels of support for democracy as a regime among women, and this pattern persists across sub-Saharan Africa (Konte and Klasen 2016) and Latin America (Walker and Kehoe 2013). Although some hypotheses for these differences are grounded in individual-level factors such as socioeconomic resources and risk aversion, the explanatory findings point toward the importance of political context, including regime change. Importantly, when Konte and Klasen 2016 control for gender discrimination at the contextual level in institutions, the gender gap in support for democracy disappears. In post-communist countries, Oakes 2002 theorizes that women may be less supportive of democracy and more supportive of the previous regime based on women's higher levels of religiosity and women's economic vulnerability in the face of a concomitant rollback of safety net policies.

A few studies find links between women's numbers in elected office and higher support for the legislature and democratic legitimacy among both men and women (Norris and Franklin 1997; Karp and Banducci 2008; Schwindt-Bayer 2018; Schwindt-Bayer and Mishler 2005). In Latin America, Schwindt-Bayer and Alles 2018 find that women's legislative representation has positive effects for men's and women's support for representative democracy and trust in legislatures. Similarly, Barnes and Jones's study of Argentina extends these effects to the provincial level, uncovering the boosting effects of women in provincial legislatures for political trust (Barnes and Jones 2018). However, women's numbers in provincial cabinets did not show similar effects for political trust.

We specifically contend that political change can reshape the contours of political connections, either bringing more people into the political process or driving them away. We focus on highly visible breaks with the past, and specifically with the role that steep jumps in the number of women officeholders can have on citizens' psychological orientations toward political processes and government. Does a political context of increased female political leadership encourage greater levels of citizen political connectedness? Will the inclusion of women into politics improve the quality of our democracies?

How Visibility Matters: The Visible Cue Theory of Representation

Scholars have argued that the very presence of women among elected officials can have far-reaching mass-level effects and increase female political participation and engagement (Liu and Banaszak 2017; Franceschet, Krook, and Piscopo 2012; Desposato and Norrander 2009; Wolbrecht and Campbell 2007; Kittilson 2005; Burns, Schlozman, and Verba 2001; Carroll 1985). Mansbridge contends that the psychological benefits of descriptive representation emanate from its ability to shape the social meaning of "ability to rule" (1999: 628), heightening the connection of group members to their government. Greater equality and inclusion among those in power may foster a sense of belonging and inclusion at the mass level.

Yet, despite the fact that we have seen staggering changes in the number of women politicians in countries across the globe, women's political engagement has largely continued to lag behind men's. These gendered differences in democratic engagement drive our central research question: how do women most effectively connect to the democratic process? Specifically, we ask whether (and *under what conditions*) the more equitable representation of women in positions of power affects women as democratic citizens.

If the absence of women from positions of political power sends the "implicit message that politics is about men—and, therefore, for men" (Verba, Burnes, and Schlozman 1997: 1064) and has the effect of discouraging women's political engagement, what happens when large numbers of women enter political office? How does the message change? And do changes in women's presence among elected officials also alter men's political engagement? Additionally, what role do gender quotas play in shaping the democratic participation of both men and women?

We argue that political connectedness is responsive to greater numbers of women in office, but only when it is noticeable. Incremental change may not matter as much as meaningful increases in women's presence in elected office, because these signify a visible break with the past, as we will explain in Chapter 2. Simply put, we find that gender gaps in political engagement are not insurmountable and that the representation of women in positions of power has real consequences for female citizens. Importantly, we find that notable jumps in the inclusion of women into politics affect the previously included group (men) differently than they affect the previously marginalized group (women).

Methodology

Despite the fact that women's presence in political office has dramatically increased over the last 15 years, we still know little about how and when women's political presence affects political engagement and support among citizens. This book explores this relationship, drawing on a cross-country analysis (using survey data from across the Latin American region) and a comprehensive examination of a single, optimal case.

Latin America is an ideal place to consider how increasing numbers of women in political office can affect political engagement and political support. First, Latin America pioneered the use of gender quotas. Second, women's numbers in office have risen precipitously in the region due to the use of these gender quotas and (more recently) due to the adoption of progressive gender parity measures that call for equal numbers of male and female candidates. Third, regular public opinion surveys have been carried out in Latin America over the last 15 years.

The use of national gender quotas—by bringing women into politics in large numbers—can substantially alter how a previously marginalized group engages in the democratic process. There are three types of affirmative action measures (reserved seats, internal party quotas, and national quotas) that have been adopted with the aim of increasing the number of women in office. Scholarship has predominantly focused on national gender quotas, which have been adopted en masse throughout Latin America (Baldez 2004; Htun and Jones 2002; Jones 1996; Krook 2004; Meier 2004). While reserved seats require that a set percentage or number of seats be set aside for women in legislative bodies, both internal party quotas and national quotas instead alter political parties' candidate selection procedures. Political parties sometimes choose to establish internal party quotas to increase women's representation or to demonstrate their commitment to gender equality (Davidson-Schmich 2016). Typically, parties determine that a set percentage of their candidacies will be filled by women. Parties have also set such affirmative action policies for internal party positions (Caul 1999). National quotas (which are sometimes referred to as legislative quotas), however, are "measures passed by national parliaments requiring that all parties nominate a certain percentage of women" (Krook and O'Brien 2010: 260). Unlike party quotas, national quotas are legally sanctioned. Currently, more than 70 countries have adopted national quotas as a "fast track" approach to increasing women's representation in politics (see Quota Project; Dahlerup and Freidenvall 2005). Gender quotas have led to sizable change in the numbers of women in politics in countries across the globe (Tripp and Kang 2008).

The Latin American region pioneered the use of these legislative quotas. Argentina adopted the first gender quota in 1991, and over the course of the next decade the majority of Latin American countries followed suit, as Table 1.2 makes clear. A handful of stragglers, such as Chile, only recently adopted gender quotas. At present, Guatemala is the only Latin American country that has not legislated a gender quota, and Venezuela does not

TABLE 1.2 Gender Quota Laws in Latin America

COUNTRY	YEAR OF INITIAL QUOTA ADOPTION	CURRENT CANDIDATE LIST RULE
Argentina	1991	Parity
Bolivia	1997	Parity
Brazil	1997	30%
Chile	2015	40%
Colombia	1998 (Repealed), 2014	30%
Costa Rica	1996	Parity
Dominican Republic	1997	33%
Ecuador	1997	Parity
El Salvador	2013	30%
Guatemala		
Honduras	2000	Parity
Mexico	2002	Parity
Nicaragua	2012	Parity
Panama	1996	Parity
Paraguay	1996	20%
Peru	1997	30%
Uruguay	2009	30%
Venezuela	1997 (Repealed)	

SOURCE: Funk, Hinojosa, and Piscopo 2017 for year of initial quota adoption; Piscopo and Wylie (forthcoming) for current candidate list rule.

currently use quotas (since the gender quota which had been adopted at the end of the 1990s was quickly repealed).

Although the application of gender quotas has led to remarkable advances in women's officeholding across the globe over the course of the last 20 years, not all quotas have been equally effective. In many countries of the region, women's numbers in congress have risen substantially due to the application of quotas, leading to parity or near-parity in Bolivia, Mexico, Nicaragua, and Costa Rica (IPU 2019). But, in countries like Brazil and Paraguay, where women's legislative representation still hovers at about 15 percent, gender quotas have proven largely ineffective. Overall, however, Latin America has seen sizable increases due to the nearly wholesale adoption of quotas across the region: women's representation in (lower or unicameral) congresses of Latin America nearly tripled during the course of just 25 years, rising from 9 percent in 1990 to 25 percent in 2014 (Htun and Piscopo 2014).

While the use of gender quotas and their successful transformation of the region's legislative bodies make Latin America worthy of study, we are able to focus on this region because LAPOP has surveyed Latin Americans for the last 15 years. These high-quality, cross-national surveys have routinely asked some of the same questions to citizens of countries from across the region and have regularly queried individuals about their political participation, political engagement, and support. While the LAPOP data allow us to carry out a cross-country analysis that tracks political engagement and support across multiple points in time, we also use our own unique survey data from Uruguay to gain greater analytical leverage over the relationship between women's representation in political positions of power and citizens' political engagement and political support.

Discerning the effects of gender quotas and women's gains in elected office requires a different survey design from what LAPOP surveys can offer. To assess change in political engagement and support, the timing of surveys is key. The ideal surveys would be slated for immediately before and immediately after an election, in order to isolate the effects of the election results themselves and due to the potential dilution of effects over time. As time after the election passes, acts of representation by elected officials can confound the influence of visible symbols of inclusion. However, large-scale public opinion surveys select survey dates based on other factors. Large-scale surveys rarely query citizens often; LAPOP tends to field its surveys about once every two years, while the Comparative Study of Electoral Systems surveys occur even less frequently. Scholars have also noted that for the types of questions that we are asking, these types of surveys may lack relevant variables, or the necessary variables may appear infrequently or only for some countries (Espírito-Santo and Verge 2017).

But additionally, and even more difficult: the surveys must be timed around an election where women's numbers in legislative office will shoot up. Knowing when and where that will happen is no small feat. The ideal methodology requires more than just appropriate survey questions and well-timed surveys. The best possibility would be for researchers to undertake such a survey in a context of few other political changes. Researchers could be stymied if the number of women in office is not the only major political change afoot. If a new political party won a majority, or a president took a turn toward authoritarianism, scholars would be unable to separate out effects due to greater levels of women in office from some of these other changes. The optimal research design would allow us to undertake surveys in a context of minimal political change, providing us the opportunity to control for other potentially confounding factors.

The Case of Uruguay

Uruguay proved an ideal laboratory in which to assess the effects of increased numbers of women in politics. Because of the ability to predict a sizable increase in women's representation, the significant gap between the adoption of the gender quota and its first use, and the single-country case design, the data that we are able to obtain from the Uruguayan case are optimal for analyzing the relationship between descriptive representation and citizens' political engagement and support.

First, the Uruguayan gender quota gave us confidence that women's descriptive representation would get a sizable bump. This created an opportunity for us to compare political engagement and political support before and after the election and thereby assess the effects of descriptive representation. Due to its clear placement mandates and enforcement mechanisms, the quota law was expected to succeed. Women's descriptive representation did increase following the 2014 elections, doubling in the Senate (surging from 12.9 percent to 25.8 percent); the results—as expected by Uruguayan experts—were less dramatic in the lower house (climbing from 15.2 percent to 18.2 percent).[7] The quota therefore served as a prognostication tool, allowing us to foresee this increase in women's descriptive representation. Typically, it is impossible to know when change will occur, and when it does occur it is usually incremental (Espírito-Santo and Verge 2017). In the Uruguayan case, however, change comes overnight and is sizable. We were able to anticipate this impressive shift in the gender composition of the legislature and time our survey to take advantage of the fact that this change would not be incremental because of the passage of the quota.

Second, the five-year lag between the adoption of the gender quota (in 2009) and its implementation for the legislative elections (2014) was fortuitous. The typical timeframe from passage of a quota to its first application is usually brief. For example, Mexico adopted a gender quota in April 2002 and utilized it in the July 2003 elections. This uncommon delay provided us with enough time to secure funding and carry out a comprehensive survey of Uruguayan citizens prior to the 2014 elections.

Finally, the use of a single-country case allows us to control for cultural, political, and institutional differences that we would otherwise encounter in a cross-country analysis. Further, Uruguay's stability—in both its

---

[7] Chapter 4 explains why the changes were largely felt in the Senate and not in the Chamber of Representatives.

political institutions and its political party system—allows us to be confident that any changes to engagement and support that our survey captured would not be the result of changes to Uruguayan institutions. For example, had we carried out this work in Chile before and after the implementation of that country's gender quota in the 2017 elections, we would have encountered a host of changes to the electoral system—including a move from a binomial system to multi-seat proportional representation and an increase in the number of seats in the legislature—that could have significant effects for how citizens view and interact with their political system. The Uruguayan case, on the other hand, proved ideal for analysis because the 2014 election did not introduce any significant political changes other than the increased role for women. Not only did the *Frente Amplio* retain control of the presidency, but it also maintained control of both chambers of parliament. The new president campaigned on a program of continuity, vowing to maintain his predecessor's agenda. The outgoing president was easily elected to a senate seat. Again, were this study to have been conducted in Chile, we would have been flummoxed by significant political changes: the repudiation of the leftist agenda of Michelle Bachelet, the rise of new political parties, and the obvious disgust among the electorate with politics as usual.

Our survey employed a unique design that was best suited for capturing the effects of increased numbers of women in legislative office on everyday Uruguayans. The timing of the two waves of the surveys was strategic. The first wave was scheduled after candidate lists were announced, since this timing should call attention to the use of a gender quota; all lists were required to comply with the new quota. The second wave was timed to begin after the results of the election were called, when news of women's increased representation in the upcoming parliament would have been disseminated. This required waiting for votes to be counted and results to be verified. The second wave needed to conclude before the new parliament was seated in order for us to see how the increased descriptive representation of women would affect citizens' political engagement and support absent any changes to policy priorities (which could be altered by an influx of female legislators). Because the newly elected parliament had not been sworn into office yet—and because the outgoing parliament was on recess from October 26 until their terms ended—any changes to political engagement *could not* be the result of changes to the substantive representation of women, i.e. the women who had been elected to parliament had not yet made any policy changes nor had any other policy changes been enacted.

This in-depth case study of Uruguay complements broader comparative data and allows us to hold constant potentially confounding influences (such as electoral system or political culture that might also affect political engagement and support for the political process). Moreover, the close timing of the surveys means that broader cultural forces cannot explain changes to political engagement or political support; namely, it is neither educational achievements among girls and women nor female labor force participation driving the changes that we see. Appendix 1.1 provides more detailed information about the survey.

In short, the Uruguayan data provides us the analytical leverage to untangle the effects of gender quotas and the subsequent increase in women's share of elected positions; we find that the latter exerts a measurable impact on political engagement and support. We also analyze (in Chapter 4) the impact of the larger political context to add confidence that the changes we see to political engagement and support are not the result of other political changes taking place in Uruguay. Longitudinal analysis within a single country is necessary to separate the effects of gender quotas and the surge in women's presence in congress from other confounding factors.

Overview of the Book

This introductory chapter sets the stage for our analysis by presenting the puzzle of female political engagement and political support: despite tremendous increases in women's political presence—as presidents, ministers, and legislators—at the mass level women remain less politically engaged than men. Moreover, this chapter frames the question motivating our study: do different forces shape men's and women's connections to the democratic process?

Chapter 2 presents our theoretical framework underpinning expectations about how increases in descriptive representation—the number of women in politics—act as symbols to elicit change in orientations toward politics, especially among women. We argue that women's inclusion fosters a sense of belonging among women in the electorate. Importantly, these cues about women's inclusion must be visible to ordinary citizens. Widespread awareness of quotas and women's numbers in elected office are key implicit assumptions in much prior research on descriptive and symbolic representation. We argue that gender quotas and women's presence in office can only yield changes in mass-level attitudes under conditions of visibility. We develop a visible cue theory of representation, linking descriptive to symbolic representation. We contend that having more women in politically powerful positions signals that politics is not strictly an arena for men (but only if citizens are aware of women's political presence).

Chapter 3 presents some challenges in testing the impact of visible gains in women's election to office for political engagement and support at the mass level. Women's gains in elected office across Latin America are, after all, embedded in the dynamics of broader election campaigns and political change. Specifically, the chapter provides in-depth examination of a set of Latin American countries where women's legislative representation doubled from one election to the next and rose above 20 percent to assess how increases in women's representation might affect political connectedness. While women's gains in elected office were substantial in each instance, these gains may not have always been visible, and cross-national survey timing makes it even more difficult to gauge the impact of these changes. In this way, this chapter highlights the necessity of employing a different type of analysis and sets up the advantage of our unique Uruguayan case.

In Chapter 4, we introduce our Uruguayan panel survey and also present data gathered from interviews with political elites conducted in Montevideo and content analyses of three major Uruguayan newspapers. Drawing on these data, we carefully demonstrate how the quota policy itself failed to attract visibility among the general population, but then show how women's gains in elected office were more visible. By establishing the visibility of women's descriptive representation following the sizable increase in women's numbers in parliament, this chapter paves the way for our empirical analyses of the Uruguayan data.

How do sizable and visible gains in women's officeholding affect women's and men's political engagement? In Chapter 5, we examine how women's presence shapes gender differences in political knowledge, interest, discussion, and citizens' beliefs about their own efficaciousness. We draw on our novel survey in Uruguay before quota implementation and after the resulting increase in women's descriptive representation to track gender differences over time. Both bivariate and multivariate analyses reveal a consistent pattern of rising engagement for women as a consequence of the changing face of descriptive representation. After the election, previously statistically significant gender gaps in favor of men's greater political engagement evaporate for political interest, political knowledge, perceptions of understanding issues, and political discussion.

In an era where many lament declining levels of political support, it is important to note that the driving forces behind political support may be gendered, albeit in subtle ways. Chapter 6 examines changes in men's and women's trust in elections, confidence in democratic institutions, and support for democracy in Uruguay. We find that the visible and sizable jump in women's election to office in Uruguay fortifies women's political connections. Before the election, there were few differences between men and women on most dimensions of political support. After the election, however, women's political support ascends higher than men's levels, and in most instances this gender gap becomes statistically significant. On balance, men's political support does not appear to change much after the election; instead, it is women who are galvanizing these changes.

The concluding chapter notes the ways that our research speaks to policy: while the passage of gender quotas may not have an effect on citizens, the resultant gains in the number of women—if visible—will. Our findings indicate that far-reaching gender gaps can be overcome by more equitable representation in our political institutions. We demonstrate that descriptive representation matters for citizen engagement with and support for the democratic process. Simply put, female citizens react to visible cues: seeing more women in political office creates greater feelings of political connection.

APPENDIX 1.1

With funding from USAID, we surveyed 1,200 Uruguayan citizens in the months immediately before and immediately after the October 2014 elections. We hired a well-regarded Uruguayan polling firm to carry out the surveys in the capital city of Montevideo; the capital city and its suburbs contain nearly half the Uruguayan population. The first wave of the panel survey consisted of face-to-face interviews lasting approximately 20 minutes, while the second wave of the survey was conducted telephonically.

Panel surveys are recognized as the best longitudinal survey method available to assess changes in attitudes. Nonetheless, their disadvantage is panel attrition. Of the original 1,200 respondents in our first wave, 731 were re-interviewed in the second wave. This second wave then included 469 new respondents who were added to address attrition issues. However, this attrition did not significantly change the composition of our sample. According to a difference of means test, the difference in the proportion of men and women participating in T1 and T2 was insignificant (F=0.32, p=.57). In T1, men comprised 46 percent of survey respondents, whereas in T2, 44 percent of those surveyed were men. Also, the type of men and women who stayed in the panel did not differ significantly. We found no gender differences for the following variables at T1 and T2: (1) education (2) ideology, (3) income, and (4) talking about politics. In addition, during T1, men were more knowledgeable than women about politics; the same was true during the second wave. We only found differences for men and women across the two waves on age (women were older than men for T2, but not for T1). In the analysis, we control for age (as well as other demographic and political variables). Similarly, people who remained in the panel were not more likely than these new respondents to know about the quota: .15 (.36) for the panel respondents at T2 and .21 (.40) for the fresh respondents included in the second wave.

The first wave established a baseline and measured the effects of the quota adoption itself (earlier data from LAPOP provided us with a pre-quota baseline), while the second wave was necessary for understanding how increases in the number of women in parliament would themselves affect political engagement and support. We designed our own panel survey to tap political engagement and political support variables. In writing the survey instrument, we relied when possible on established measures and previously used questions in order to facilitate comparisons with other studies on this topic.

By designing our own survey, we also are able to deal with one other confounding issue. As others have noted, "researchers will find separating the effects of women's presence from the effects of the quota particularly difficult" (Franceschet, Krook, and Piscopo 2012: 18), but this is something that we addressed head on by strategically timing our surveys (and by using prior LAPOP surveys in Uruguay as baseline measures for our variables of interest). We deviated from traditional survey questions used by the World Values Survey and LAPOP by also attempting to assess visibility of the gender quota and of women's representation in politics. We asked our respondents about the gender quota and women's representation. Our survey additionally asked questions about media usage, in an effort to understand how information regarding the use of a gender quota or increased numbers of women in politics could be spread and understood by citizens.

CHAPTER 2 | How Visibility Matters
The Visible Cue Theory of Representation

One of the principles associated with legal judgments is that justice
must not only be done but be seen to be done. By the same token, we
might well say that representatives must not only be representative but
also be seen to be so.

—Phillips 1995: 79–80

DOES REPRESENTATION REQUIRE that the representative be seen, as Phillips
suggests? In this chapter, we theorize that to understand the dynamics of
the complex relationships between descriptive, substantive, and symbolic
representation—as well as the possible impact of gender quotas—we must
look at the role that visibility can play. We build on existing theories of
descriptive and symbolic representation to propose a visible cue theory
of representation—one that examines how changes in the composition of
elected officials can signal inclusion in the process of representation, ultimately enhancing democracy.

We focus on the link between changes in descriptive representation
and symbolic representation. We argue that visible changes in the holistic makeup of representatives alter the connections between citizens
and the democratic process. The composition of the elected body sends
people signals about who belongs in politics and who does not. The political arena, both at the elite and mass levels, has long been dominated by
men. Women's advancements in these representative bodies empower the
represented. Specifically, visible jumps in women's numbers among legislative representatives foster a sense of belonging among women in the
electorate.

Seeing Women, Strengthening Democracy. Magda Hinojosa and Miki Caul Kittilson, Oxford University Press (2020).
© Oxford University Press. DOI: 10.1093/oso/9780197526941.001.0001.

Three Interrelated Strands of Representation

Political representation refers to three conceptually distinct elements: descriptive representation, substantive representation, and symbolic representation (Pitkin 1967). First, when we discuss the increased numbers of women in political office, we are referring to women's descriptive representation. A legislative body with greater descriptive representation more accurately reflects the demographic characteristics of the population that it represents. Second, substantive representation refers to the representation of group interests. Scholars concerned with women's substantive representation focus on understanding whether women's policy preferences are being advanced. Third, symbolic representation refers to feelings and attitudes that are evoked by political symbols. While we elaborate on the interrelated nature of descriptive, substantive, and symbolic representation, the primary focus of our work is on only a portion of the complex and integrated structure of representation.

Descriptive representation is all too often "considered to be of value if it manages to contribute to the substantive representation of women and improve the consideration of women's different needs and interests" (Lombardo and Meier 2014: 120). As Jane Mansbridge explains, "The primary function of representative democracy is to represent the substantive interests of the represented through both deliberation and aggregation. Descriptive representation should be judged primarily on this criterion" (Mansbridge 1999: 630). It is therefore not surprising that much academic work has studied the relationship between women's descriptive representation and their substantive representation, with the assumption that as more women enter representative bodies, women's interests are more likely to be represented. Taken as a whole, these studies indicate that greater numbers of women in office do lead to the greater substantive representation of women. While the inclusion of ever greater numbers of women into legislative bodies enhances the substantive representation of women in the policy process (see, for example, Thomas 1991; Burrell 1997; Celis 2006; Tremblay and Pelletier 2000; Schwindt-Bayer 2006), it does not necessarily lead to greater substantive representation as measured by policy outcomes (see, for example, Weldon 2002).[1]

Scholars have also analyzed the relationship between substantive representation and symbolic representation. Schwindt-Bayer and Mishler find

---

[1] Franceschet and Piscopo 2008 explain mixed findings within this literature by distinguishing policy as process from policy as outcome.

that substantive representation has little effect on female citizen's views of legislative legitimacy, and the factor that may drive these results is limited information. Citizens may simply be unaware of policy changes: "Given the low levels of political knowledge characteristic of citizens in most democratic polities, many citizens simply may not have the knowledge to accurately judge the policy responsiveness of the system" (Schwindt-Bayer and Mishler 2005: 421).

The relationship between descriptive representation and symbolic representation seems innate; many of us simply expect that when an individual from a historically underrepresented group sees someone who "looks like them" in a position of power, it changes political attitudes and behaviors and alters how that individual views her own government and its democratic institutions.[2] As Mansbridge explains, "Seeing proportional numbers of members of their group exercising the responsibility of ruling with full status in the legislature can enhance de facto legitimacy by making citizens, and particularly members of historically underrepresented groups, feel as if they themselves were present in the deliberations" (Mansbridge 1999: 650).

For those who have largely been outside of politics, the presence of descriptive representatives may serve to encourage individuals to similarly engage with the political process. The role modeling that comes from this descriptive representation can be crucial for mobilizing political interest among members of that group (Dovi 2002: 730, fn 6). Greater numbers of women in politics may function as symbols signaling that politics is for women and not just for men. The political exclusion of women and others from politics "create[s] the meaning that Blacks and women cannot rule, or are not suitable for rule" (Mansbridge 1999: 649), and it is only the inclusion of these groups into politics that can provide a countervailing message.[3]

---

[2] There is also a rich literature that examines the symbolic effects of the descriptive representation of historically underrepresented racial and ethnic minorities. Where African Americans are represented by black mayors, they are more likely to participate politically, are more politically knowledgeable, and display more trust in public officials (Bobo and Gilliam 1990). Gay found that African Americans are more willing to contact their representatives when those representatives are themselves African American (Gay 2002: 726).

[3] Phillips argues that a lack of political interest among some is not in itself problematic since "the interest in politics is unevenly distributed, as is the interest in sport or in jazz," but that when "levels of participation and involvement have coincided too closely with differences by class or gender or ethnicity" then we can assume that this is a problem of political inequality (Phillips 1995: 32).

Political elites are aware of this connection between the presence of an underrepresented group and feelings of political inclusion. That women's presence in elected office may serve as a symbol of inclusion and democracy is supported by Valdini's 2019 work on the strategic calculations of political elites. Taken together, evidence from several cases supports the idea that established powerholders facilitate women's entrance into elected office when they perceive it will benefit the party electorally. Stereotypically feminine personality traits such as inclusiveness and honesty potentially benefit parties and their leaders in the aftermath of declining public support or scandals.

While many have argued that the presence of female representatives can have transformative effects and send powerful messages at the mass level (Alexander 2012; Wolbrecht and Campbell 2007; Campbell and Wolbrecht 2006; Kittilson 2005; Paxton and Hughes 2007; Barnes and Burchard 2013; Burns, Schlozman, and Verba 2001; Carroll 1985; Reingold 2000; Carroll 1994), studies have not always confirmed this positive relationship. The literature examining the effects of descriptive representation on symbolic representation has been less than conclusive.

Some studies document that female candidates and legislators heighten women's political engagement.[4] Examining the United States, High-Pippert and Comer find that when women are represented by a woman, they are more likely to participate in politics and to feel knowledgeable and efficacious (1998: 60–61). For Latin America, Desposato and Norrander find that the gender gap in political participation was smaller in those countries where women had higher rates of political representation, and they predicted that the gender gap in participation would be entirely eliminated when legislative seats were equally distributed between men and women (2009: 157). Schwindt-Bayer 2010 finds that both men and women were more satisfied with government and expressed greater trust in congress when women held more seats in the legislative body. Similarly, Schwindt-Bayer and Mishler find that "the impact of female legislators accelerates as their numbers in the legislature grow" and that women's confidence in legislatures (which they use as a proxy for symbolic representation) does increase due to descriptive representation (2005: 422). Women's presence enhances people's confidence in representative bodies;

---

[4] Mansbridge 1999 and Phillips 1995 both point to the fact that the very presence of female politicians could alter views about women's proper place and that this in itself is reason to elect more women to politics. Indeed, Alexander 2012 finds that increased female representation contributes to more positive attitudes about women's abilities to govern.

recent experimental work indicates that this is the case even when the issue that is being debated or discussed is unrelated to gender (Clayton, O'Brien, and Piscopo 2019).[5]

Analogous work that analyzes female descriptive representation outside of legislative bodies has come to the same conclusions. Alexander and Jalalzai 2020 find that male and female citizens in countries that have recently had female heads of state have greater levels of political interest, and Reyes-Housholder and Schwindt-Bayer (2016) find that having a woman president makes female citizens more politically participatory. Recently, Liu and Banaszak 2017 examine role model effects based on the proportion of female cabinet members. Women are more likely to vote, join parties, sign petitions, and peacefully demonstrate (but not engage in strikes or boycotts) in countries with more women in cabinets.

However, others have not found these same effects (Lawless 2004; Dolan 2006; Kittilson and Schwindt-Bayer 2010). For example, across several Latin American countries with female presidents, Jalalzai 2015 found little effect for social trust, political interest, or satisfaction with democracy. Looking at legislatures, Karp and Banducci find that the presence of more women in elected office does not lead to greater political engagement among women, although they did find that where there are more women in office, citizens "are more likely to be satisfied with the way democracy works and more likely to believe that elections reflect the views of voters" (Karp and Banducci 2008: 112). In their examination of subnational positions, Barnes and Jones find that higher numbers of women in cabinet positions in Argentina do not lead to greater trust in government (2018).

The Role of Gender Quotas: More than Just a Gateway to Descriptive Representation?

Studies of gender quotas predominantly focus on developments to the descriptive representation of women as a consequence of quota adoption. While some attention has also been paid to examining how gender quotas affect women's substantive representation (see for example, Schwindt-Bayer 2010; Franceschet and Piscopo 2008; Zetterberg 2008; Devlin and

---

[5] Interestingly, the authors find that even anti-feminist decisions are perceived to be more legitimate when women have been represented equally in the decision-making bodies (Clayton, O'Brien, and Piscopo 2019: 127).

Elgie 2008), few scholars have focused on understanding the impact of gender quotas on symbolic representation.

Although some suggest that quotas can "reshape attitudes, values, and ideas towards women's roles in politics" (Kittilson 2005: 29), scholars that have empirically tested this relationship have rarely found such a positive impact.[6] For instance, Zetterberg 2009 found that quotas did not intensify female citizens' trust in politicians or in political parties in Latin America. Looking at 18 Latin American countries, Morgan and Buice 2013 found no effects from gender quota laws. Similarly, in their analysis of Uruguay, Kittilson and Schwindt-Bayer 2012 scrutinized the relationship between quotas and symbolic representation. Using Americas Barometer data from both before 2008 and after 2010 quota adoption (but before implementation), they found minimal impact on political knowledge, political interest, or political participation.[7]

Why might quotas not boost political engagement or trust? Past research suggests several potential reasons. Both Morgan and Buice 2013 and Kittilson and Schwindt-Bayer 2012 theorize that timing matters, but based on opposing rationales. On the one hand, Morgan and Buice believe that it might be because most quota laws had been adopted a decade earlier. In other words, they believe too much time has elapsed since the quotas were implemented. On the other hand, Kittilson and Schwindt-Bayer suggest that the reason they do not find the expected results is because in the Uruguayan case, quotas had too recently been adopted. They propose that there might be a delay in mobilization that comes with quotas, "requiring a longer period of political learning" (Kittilson and

---

[6] Quotas might instead have the opposite effect. Rather than increase political interest or participation in the political process, quotas could have a backlash effect. Clayton 2015 found that quotas were seen as exclusionary and unfair when applied to community councils in Lesotho, and had no positive effects on political engagement. The application of those gender quotas, though, meant barring all men from running in quota districts because of the use of single-member districts. Quotas are more regularly used in conjunction with list systems, and therefore men and women appear on ballots. Burnet 2011, when examining the case of Rwanda, also found negative attitudes among men that were associated with the quota and found evidence of resentment. As Lombardo and Meier 2014 explain, "To gender quota opponents, the state is doing something it is not supposed to do, namely creating equal outcomes, whereas the role of the state is limited to creating equal opportunities. Gender quotas, then here stand for the violation of equality in that they introduce the principle of positive discrimination or, put differently state-organised discrimination" (134).

[7] They focus on the time period prior to implementation since they attempt to assess the effects of the quota itself. While it could be that the quota did not directly influence symbolic representation, another possibility is that there was little awareness of the quota. Absent visibility of the gender quota, the quota would have almost no effects on citizen attitudes. We explore this possibility directly in Chapter 4, and build on the work of Kittilson and Schwindt-Bayer by looking at democratic engagement both after passage of the gender quota and after its implementation.

Schwindt-Bayer 2012: 129). In the Uruguayan case, the quota had not yet been implemented.

Alternatively, as Kittilson and Schwindt-Bayer explain, "it may simply be that quotas often have the effect they are designed to have—increase the representation of women in political office—but their effects are limited to just that. Although activists and scholars have suggested that quotas could have a wide range of consequences, it may be that the effects of quotas are much more limited" (Kittilson and Schwindt-Bayer 2012: 124). But, Zetterberg suggests other possibilities: (1) women might "question their government's true com mitment to gender equality"; (2) gender quotas may have failed to alter nomination procedures; and (3) people might not know about quota laws (Zetterberg 2009: 725). His first possibility raises the notion that citizens may not respond to a cue that they view cynically; if citizens believe that quotas have been adopted by elites for self-serving purposes rather than due to a true commitment to gender equality, quotas will not send the same message and therefore will not have the same effect. The second possibility also indicates a concern about the type of message being sent; if nomination procedures have not changed, the message being transmitted may be that the status quo prevails. Most importantly, Zetterberg's final suggestion about a lack of knowledge of the quota speaks to how awareness of the quota is essential to changing public perceptions. We focus on this awareness in building our visible cue theory of representation.

The Visible Cue Theory of Representation

> Seeing women from the U.S. House of Representatives storming the
> steps of the Senate, for example, made some women feel actively
> represented in ways that a photograph of male legislators could never
> have done.
>
> —Mansbridge 1999: 651

Our visible cue theory of representation links descriptive to symbolic representation. We contend that perceptible changes are key to understanding the effects of greater gender equality among elected representatives in the political arena. We maintain that having more women in elected office will have little influence on citizens if they are unaware of increases in women's presence. In short, absent visibility, we expect that heightened descriptive representation will fail to exert symbolic effects; changes to substantive representation when unknown will produce little consequence for political engagement or support; and quotas will not lead to greater symbolic representation if no one knows about them.

The visible cue theory brings visibility into the spotlight. While visibility has often been given short shrift in studies of women's representation, some scholars have introduced the concept of visibility in their own work on symbolic representation.[8] Scholars have explained that "the mere presence of a female politician is not enough: the degree to which the candidacy is visible—either as a function of the office sought, the viability of the candidate, or the extent to which attention is drawn to the unique phenomenon of female politicians—creates a context in which women's presence as politicians can affect the political engagement of women" (Campbell and Wolbrecht 2006: 235). We build on this existing literature to develop the concept of visibility and understand its effects on symbolic representation.

First, we deviate from other scholars in explicitly separating the concept of visibility from viability. Political scientists have largely used viability as a stand-in for visibility. The viable cue theory, elaborated by Lonna Rae Atkeson, argues that "the simple presence or absence of a 'like' candidate is not enough to increase political engagement. Instead . . . 'like' candidates must be viable for an increase in political engagement to occur" (Atkeson 2003: 1041). This viable cue theory is premised, like much of the American politics literature examining the relationship between descriptive representation and symbolic representation, on candidacies, with an expectation that having viable candidacies will send an important political message to citizens about who does and does not belong in politics. Or, as Atkeson states, "The cues provided by minimal female representation in politics and campaigns are that women are not full citizens and that they are not welcome in the political world" (Atkeson 2003: 1053). Campbell

---

[8] See, for example, excellent work by Koch 1997; Hansen 1997; Sapiro and Conover 1997; Burns, Schlozman, and Verba 2001; Atkeson 2003; Schwindt-Bayer and Mishler 2005; Campbell and Wolbrecht 2006; Atkeson and Carrillo 2007; Ulbig 2007; Zetterberg 2009; Morgan and Buice 2013; Jalalzai 2015; Liu and Banaszak 2017; Hinojosa, Fridkin, and Kittilson 2017; Alexander and Jalalzai 2020; Barnes and Taylor-Robinson 2018; and Beauregard 2018. Ulbig 2007 tests whether trust in municipal government rises based on the percentage of women serving on municipal legislative bodies for men versus women, finding a slightly positive relationship for women and the opposite (and stronger) effect for men. Importantly, awareness (which we term visibility) moderates this relationship. Ulbig actually tests for awareness by asking: "How closely do you follow news about local politics and government?" To assess visibility fully, we believe that the question utilized must more closely ask about knowledge of women's representation in local politics.

and Wolbrecht go further, explicitly linking visibility to viability. They explain that, "Visibility suggests that a woman's campaign is sufficiently viable and the office sufficiently important that the woman is viewed as a credible politician, rather than as powerless, not serious, or a token" (Campbell and Wolbrecht 2006: 235). We extend the concept of visibility by separating it from viability.

Equating visibility with viability is problematic. For a candidate to be visible, she must be seen. People must know that she is running for office. Perhaps they will see her campaign advertisements on television. Maybe they will hear her speak at an event. Closed-list proportional represen tation is common in countries across the globe. Parties not only select and rank their candidates in this type of system, but parties also control campaign propaganda, which typically features only a photo of the top candidate and a group shot of all others (Clucas and Valdini 2015). For a candidate to be viable, on the other hand, she must be slated by the party for an electable spot on its list. If the candidate is in one of those spots, she will be elected, even if she is unknown to those people who will soon be her constituents. A viable candidate, therefore, may not be a visible candidate, and a candidate who has somehow obtained media attention (and hence visibility) might be placed too low on a party list to have a chance of winning. To understand visibility, we must detach it from viability.

Second, we separate the concept of visibility from its routine applica-tion to candidacies. By conflating visibility with viability, scholars have ultimately confined visibility to candidates. The concept, we argue, is broadly applicable. Certainly, other scholars have also used visibility to apply to elected officeholders. For example, Schwindt-Bayer and Mishler extend visibility to legislators when they write about "a visible presence of women in the legislature" having the ability to "enhance women's confidence in the legislative process. The hypothesis is that constituents are more likely to identify with the legislature and to defer its decisions to the extent that they perceive a significant percentage of 'people like themselves' in the legislature" (2005: 413). We further argue that the con-cept can be applied both to elected or appointed politicians, as Liu and Banaszak (2017) and Barnes and Taylor-Robinson (2018) do when they write of cabinet members.

Third, we divorce visibility from dyadic representation, arguing that this concept can also be applied to collective representation. Due to the prominence of scholarship on American politics, visibility has often been applied dyadically. However, comparativists examining the relationship between descriptive representation and symbolic representation have largely focused on collective representation rather than dyadic representation; in other words, the focus has been on looking at how the percentage of women in the legislature affects symbolic representation rather than on examining the relationship between a single representative (or candidate) and a citizen. In the context of comparative politics, this relationship of collective representation is sensible. Where multi-member districts exist, it is hard to imagine a dyadic relationship between a citizen and her representative. Where all representatives are elected from a single list, who represents any one individual? We follow comparative researchers (e.g., Desposato and Norrander 2009; Schwindt-Bayer and Mishler 2005; Liu and Banaszak 2017; Wolbrecht and Campbell 2007) in analyzing the effects of collective descriptive representation on symbolic representation.

Not only is collective representation more appropriate in comparative politics, but it is also particularly impactful on how citizens perceive the legislative body. In this way, representation rests not just with one legislator, but rather with the composition of the legislative body. Claudine Gay explains how citizens may perceive the descriptive characteristics of a legislator; these may "speak volumes about her priorities and accessibility, factors that can influence the member–constituent relationship and can endear an individual legislator to her constituents, while offering no guarantees about the efficiency or outputs of a legislative process in which the preferences of hundreds of political actors must be taken into account" (Gay 2002: 730). This potential to affect perception may be even stronger when the symbol is a collective group of elected officials.

Fourth, we extend the concept of visibility from people to include policies. Policies too can be visible or invisible (widely known or generally unnoticed). We are particularly interested in how gender quota policies can either be visible or go unnoticed.

The literature on symbolic representation has often assumed visibility. We argue that visibility should not regularly be assumed but should instead be empirically tested. The mixed findings concerning the effects of women's greater descriptive representation on symbolic representation may be an artifact of these assumptions of visibility.

Assumptions of visibility are appropriate in the literature on women presidents. Jalalzai theorizes that "based on their visibility, women presidents may increase women's political participation and engagement and make them feel that the system is more democratic and responsive" (Jalalzai 2015: 11). Alexander and Jalalzai (2020) also specifically note that presidents and prime ministers are highly visible figures, and that citizens are more likely to know their presidents or prime ministers than will know the percentage of women legislators or the number of women in the cabinet. Given the outsize visibility of heads of state, citizens are more likely to know their heads of state than be aware of the number of female senators.

But assumptions of visibility, however, extend beyond presidents and prime ministers and are also applied to local council members, legislators, cabinet members, and others. For example, Atkeson and Carrillo assume that citizens will be aware of women's representation: "We argue that citizens are probably more or less aware of the gender composition of their state legislatures. Certainly few citizens know the exact proportion of women in their statehouses, but more women in office increases the general activity level by elite women, and therefore more women are visible political players" (Atkeson and Carrillo 2007: 84).

Given the difficulties of assessing visibility, some scholars have treaded cautiously (and analyzed only those positions which are likely to gain prominence). Liu and Banaszak 2017 contend that women in politics elicit greater political participation when their visibility allows them to be noticed by ordinary citizens: "Indeed, women in political office are only likely to serve as role models or create a substantive effect that inspires action by others to the extent that they are visible enough to be noticed by ordinary citizens in the first place" (Liu and Banaszak 2017: 135). They focus on cabinet ministers, arguing that these are as visible as, if not more visible than, legislators.[9] Similarly, Barnes and Taylor-Robinson also highlight the importance of visibility in their work on the effects of women in cabinets for citizen satisfaction and confidence in government. Notably, they focus their analysis on only the top-level cabinet posts, explaining that their work "is predicated on the assumption that when women hold the very top posts in the cabinet, citizens will be more likely to be aware of their appointment" (Barnes and Taylor-Robinson 2018: 237).[10]

---

[9] They also explain that, "Even when female cabinet ministers are not highly visible prior to their entry into the cabinet, the limited size of most cabinets and the small number of cabinet ministers placed at the head of parts of the bureaucracy increase a woman politician's visibility" (Liu and Banaszak 2017: 138).

[10] Like Barnes and Taylor-Robinson, Alexander and Jalalzai via their examination of women prime ministers and presidents are focusing on some of the most heavily masculine positions. "Seeing women at the helm of the most 'masculine' of domains sends important messages about women belonging in the political sphere" (Alexander and Jalalzai 2020: 25). Interestingly, in their analysis of 58 countries using multiple waves of World Values Survey data, Barnes and Taylor-Robinson find that both men and women are more likely to be satisfied with government when there are women occupying top cabinet positions.

Visibility has often been taken for granted, or, given measurement difficulties, it has been assumed. These assumptions, however, need to be questioned.[11] Some positions by their very nature are more visible than others (president vs. state legislator). Some types of representation will be more difficult to assess than others. We can expect that a citizen either does or does not know that their governor is a woman, but we cannot expect that citizens will know what proportion of senators are women. The concept of visibility then must be more finely attuned, allowing for the fact that while citizens may not know just how many female senators there are, they may nonetheless have implicitly picked up on the presence or absence of women politicians, and that they will notice meaningful change in women's descriptive representation.

How does women's descriptive representation or the passage of gender quotas become visible?[12] First, the news media are essential to creating visibility. The media may cover the passage and implementation of a gender quota in depth, or may gloss over it. The media may spend significant time describing differences in the demographic composition of an incoming legislature and, in doing so, the public would become aware of women's greater descriptive representation. Similarly, policy changes may receive either a little or a lot of media attention.[13] The media are likely to focus on substantial changes, since these will be seen as more newsworthy. Images from news media may be especially adept at crafting visibility, as

[11] Schwindt-Bayer and Reyes-Housholder 2017 explicitly choose to study the effects of increased female descriptive representation among executives rather than legislatures, in part because "citizens are more likely to know the sex of an executive than the overall percentage of a representative body that is female or even the sex of their own legislative representative" (2017: 376). Schwindt-Bayer and Reyes-Housholder use experiments to determine whether the descriptive representation of women on its own has different effects than the novelty of being the "first." Specifically, their experiment focuses on the existence of a hypothetical female governor in Brazil. They find that a hypothetical female governor leads to increased symbolic representation for women on a variety of measures (attitudes, engagement, activity) but has only positive effects on men's expected attitudes. They find that a "first" female governor does not produce more positive results. Simien's theory of symbolic empowerment also focuses on "historic firsts," arguing, however, that these historic firsts have outsized symbolic effects on citizens from the underrepresented groups (Simien 2015).

[12] Campbell and Wolbrecht also note that there are other scenarios in which women candidates can become visible: due to the office pursued (a presidential run), or if "gender itself is salient." They provide examples of this, such as "when a woman's candidacy is viewed as unique or unusual (e.g., the first time a woman pursues or wins an office), when gender is central to the campaign or agenda, or when attention is otherwise drawn to women in political life" (Campbell and Wolbrecht 2006: 235).

[13] Media framing matters for perceptions of gender quotas, too. Experimental work from Spain and Portugal finds that when quotas are framed positively, evaluations of the political system are more positive. Negative framing of the gender quotas, however, led to decreased satisfaction with democracy (Verge, Espírito-Santo, and Wiesehomeier 2015).

they allow citizens to see a change in the composition of their legislative bodies. We expect that people who pay more attention to the news media may be more influenced by changes in the representational process. These individuals will be more likely to know about the gender quota and more likely to recognize the concomitant changes to the composition of the legislature.[14] Second, transformations to communication processes and the rise of the internet have also allowed for sharing of this type of information through social media. The use of these new media allows the spread of information without the application of typical standards of newsworthiness. We can see that a message posted on Twitter gains traction and is re-tweeted again and again. Social media can be an agent for introducing this type of knowledge. Third, visibility can also spread through word of mouth. Excitement can build and be communicated from person to person in the course of everyday conversations taking place at work or school or in our homes.

Newness—"a substantial increase in the number and proportion of women elected for the first time"—may increase visibility (Beckwith 2007: 38). Past research has often focused on numerical thresholds (see Kanter 1977), especially via the concept of a critical mass, to explain links between women's descriptive and substantive representation. However, our focus is not simply on a numerical threshold but rather on change—dramatic change—since it is likely to garner attention.

Small, incremental change matters, but big, sudden shifts grab attention. Given our concern with visibility, in this book we focus on big jumps in women's political presence when examining the relationship between descriptive representation and symbolic representation. We argue that these sudden shifts are more visible: seeing women's presence in congress double overnight attracts notice, whereas seeing the percentage of women in office rise by five percentage points per election does not yield the same result. For example, in the United States, 1992 was seen as a critical year for women's representation and was dubbed the "Year of the Woman." Women's representation in the country's elected bodies has continued to rise, but rarely obtains attention like that initial significant increase. We explain our focus on big jumps as markers of visibility in greater detail in Chapter 3.

While we utilize the visible cue theory to primarily explain changes in the relationship between descriptive and symbolic representation, the

---

[14] The importance of media usage for understanding what people learn about politics has been well documented (see Zaller and Feldman 1992).

theory itself can be more broadly applied, potentially encompassing not just changes to the percentage of women in legislative bodies but also greater descriptive representation due to the election of female presidents, the appointment of cabinet ministers, or a surge in female candidacies. We explain that the passage of certain types of legislation (such as gender quotas) could have similar effects.

In this book, however, we focus on change in the gender composition of the legislature itself and expect that a similar logic applies to other decision-making bodies such as presidential cabinets. We believe that the question of whether similar effects can emerge from the election or selection of a single individual, as for the presidency, is an empirical question. Part of our theory rests on the assumption that women's inclusion in legislatures normalizes the presence and participation of women in politics, and therefore, a single officeholder may not have similar normalizing effects but may instead be perceived as a token.

How Visibility Matters to Representation

> Why are codes so important, and culture so important to political
> representation? Bear in mind the fact that a representation, a political
> claim, is nothing if it is not heard, seen, or read by its intended
> audience, those whom it is meant to attract and convince.
>
> —Saward 2006: 312

> Now when I travel, a bunch of girls tell me: "I want to be a
> candidate, too."
>
> —Ofelia Fernández, youngest member of the Buenos Aires legislature
> (Sánchez Díez 2019: np)

Figure 2.1 demonstrates the relationships that exist between descriptive, substantive, and symbolic representation. Descriptive representation is positioned at the center of the figure. Traditionally, scholars have "assessed women's descriptive representation via a head-count (simply tallying numbers of women in office)" (Hinojosa, Carle, and Woodall 2018). We take descriptive representation as our starting point, as our primary interest is to explain the effects caused by changes to descriptive representation. The top right-hand section of Figure 2.1 focuses on substantive representation. Here, the box for substantive representation is

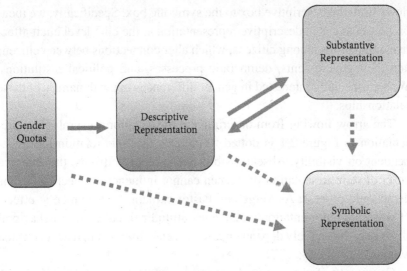

FIGURE 2.1 The Dynamics of Representation

shaded to indicate that we do not examine substantive representation in this project.

The arrow flowing from the descriptive to the substantive box in Figure 2.1 demonstrates the relationship between descriptive and substantive representation; as Pitkin explained, "they care about its composition precisely because they expect the composition to determine the activities" (Pitkin 1967: 63). Some previous studies find that when more women are in office, more women-friendly policies are enacted. We add a second arrow that flows from the substantive box to the descriptive box to indicate that substantive representation can affect descriptive representation. For example, a new law mandating the use of gender quotas (or in earlier periods, legislation granting women's suffrage) could have a powerful effect on descriptive representation.

The focus of this book lies at the bottom right-hand section of the figure: symbolic representation. Fewer studies analyze the relationship between descriptive and symbolic representation. In pioneering work, Sapiro theorized that increasing the numbers of women in politics would "affect powerful symbolic changes in politics" (Sapiro 1981: 712). Women in office will act as a symbol for women in the electorate, enhancing their connection with government and increasing women citizens' beliefs that they can influence the system. This book examines the links between descriptive and symbolic representation; our attention centers on the arrow that flows from the descriptive box to the symbolic box. Specifically, we focus on how changes in descriptive representation at the elite level elicit affective orientations among citizens, which alter connections between citizens and their governments, democratic processes, and political institutions. We are especially interested in gender differences in the dynamics of these relationships.

The arrow flowing from descriptive representation to symbolic representation in Figure 2.1 is dotted to indicate that this relationship is dependent on visibility. Absent visibility to ordinary citizens, the enlarged descriptive representation of women cannot influence connections to the democratic process. As Verge and Pastor explain, "The symbolic effects of women's representation on citizens' attitudinal, cultural, or behavioral shifts may thus largely depend on how citizens observe and react to elected women" (2018: 27).

Conversely, if changes in descriptive representation are largely invisible, we do not expect that citizens will feel more politically engaged. As Beauregard explains, "If women are not aware that they have representation in the political process and that this representation has consequences, it is unlikely that women's representation can have a positive effect on women's levels of political participation" (2018: 241).

The visible cue theory of representation argues that visible cues send a signal to women that politics is not just for men. This signal spurs women's attention to politics, making them more politically engaged citizens, but it also affects women's political support. Women become more supportive of their governments and political processes due to this message of inclusivity. Women are more willing to trust and have confidence in systems and processes that value them as full and equal citizens.

While our attention will largely focus on women's political representation in legislative bodies, the descriptive representation that is referenced in Figure 2.1 could take a variety of forms. Descriptive representation is not solely legislative numbers, but could take the form of female presidents, a significant number of women in ministerial positions, representation in other types of political posts, or a combination of these things. The visible cue theory does not limit the form that descriptive representation takes.[15]

The relationship between substantive and symbolic representation is also visually represented in Figure 2.1. Although we do not focus in

_____

[15] Nonetheless, we argue that these are empirical questions that must be tested.

this book on substantive representation, here too we expect that visibility plays an important role in whether or not substantive representation affects symbolic representation. The arrow flowing from substantive representation to symbolic representation shows this. Citizens who are often unaware of policy changes—for example, an intensified focus on women's issues in the policy process or in real changes to policy—will not experience positive changes in symbolic representation. A policy change may be visible under a variety of circumstances: an ugly debate process that receives outsize media attention, a policy with enormous reach (for example, nationalizing banks), or perhaps a catch-phrase that becomes popular ("Read my lips: no new taxes"). Simply stated, without a general or even amorphous understanding that policy changes are afoot, citizens are unlikely to change how they view and interact with their government. For this reason, the arrow flowing from substantive representation to symbolic representation is dotted.

As Figure 2.1 demonstrates, the introduction of a quota law can serve as the primary causal factor influencing descriptive representation. While quotas are designed to swell the descriptive representation of women, the application of gender quotas may influence not only descriptive representation, but also symbolic representation. Gender quotas may send important signals (Dahlerup 2006; Krook 2010). The adoption of quotas may indicate to citizens—and perhaps especially to female citizens—that their government promotes inclusivity and values women's knowledge and participation. The cue provided by the use of a gender quota differs from the cue that comes simply from increased numbers of women in office: the former could be more meaningful, given that it indicates not just that political parties have opted to run more female candidates but that the government insists on greater equality. Such a message could improve citizen perceptions and trust in government (Vincent 2004; Kittilson 2005; Schwindt-Bayer 2010) and ultimately encourage political participation (Zetterberg 2009). (Alternatively, the message could be interpreted in a negative light, indicating that the rules unfairly promote one group over another.)

Therefore, it would not be surprising that the adoption of quotas may strengthen women's connections to their political system, increasing their engagement with political goings-on, heightening their trust in governmental institutions, and augmenting their satisfaction with the political system. We argue that these effects can only happen in the context of visible gender quotas, which is why Figure 2.1 includes a dotted line between gender quotas and symbolic representation. If people are unaware of the quota, the quota can have no effects on symbolic representation. Yet, most scholarship analyzing the effects of quotas on symbolic representation presumes widespread knowledge of gender quotas. But, as Zetterberg noted in finding a lack of effect of gender quotas in the Mexican states, this may be due to lack of awareness of the quota (2009: 76). As Figure 2.1 demonstrates, the effects of gender quotas are conditional on the visibility of a gender quota. The visibility of a gender quota must be tested.[16]

As the figure shows, the effects of gender quotas might not be direct, but instead work indirectly through descriptive representation. When gender quota policies alter the composition of the national legislature, substantive policy changes may result. Thus, the quota may not affect symbolic representation directly and work only through descriptive representation.[17]

Are the Effects Similar for Younger Women?

The most important impact that you have is on the younger generations of women . . . having a whole generation of young women that saw for the first time . . . a woman seated in the presidential chair.

—Laura Chinchilla, former President of Costa Rica, *Vital Voices* panel, Arizona State University, November 5, 2019

Will seeing more women in political office affect all women similarly? We argue that women will generally become more politically engaged and more politically supportive as a result of seeing more women in politics. However, we do not discount the possibility that not all women will be affected similarly.[18] Neither men nor women are a monolithic group, and many important identities and backgrounds intersect with gender, often in complex ways. Even as women's numbers in elected office increase, it is not automatic that the diversity among women will follow.

---

[16] As Chapter 4 will make clear, the gender quota lacked visibility in Uruguay. However, we remain agnostic about the visibility of gender quotas in countries other than Uruguay. While the limited survey work indicates that citizens remain largely unaware of the existence of gender quotas, it is possible that quotas could garner significant visibility in some contexts.

[17] Barnes and Burchard 2013 state that quotas alone will not affect symbolic representation because quotas have not always resulted in an increased number of women in office. Therefore, they believe that gender quotas and increased descriptive representation must be linked.

[18] Despite our interest in intersectional issues, we are not able to test whether Afro-Uruguayan or indigenous Uruguayan women are affected due to the very low numbers of black or indigenous Uruguayans in the survey.

The empirical chapters in this book control for a number of factors, including level of education, income, political ideology, and others. We are especially interested in how age might affect citizens. A suddenly more gender equitable legislature may also exert a differential impact for younger people among the electorate (Wolbrecht and Campbell 2017). In particular, the greatest changes in connection to the political process might be found among young women. Absent years of experience and entrenched patterns, younger citizens' attitudes and orientations may be more malleable to change. Individuals in their formative years may be moved more quickly when new political events take place. Moreover, young women's sense of exclusion from the political process may not be as deeply held because they have, by definition, experienced fewer elections. While Dassonneville and McAllister 2018 do not find that higher levels of women's presence affect gender gaps in political knowledge in the short term, they do find long-term effects. In particular, with regard to political knowledge, women's presence in elected office seems to have the strongest effects for those 18–21 years old across a set of industrialized democracies. These findings support the effects of early political socialization.

In contrast, Fraile and Gomez 2017b find that gender equality cues boost the political interest of older women to a greater degree than younger women. In this way, some contextual changes can alter deeply embedded processes of gender socialization built over decades. Therefore, we will separately assess the ways that young men and young women, in particular, respond to large jumps in women's presence among elected officials.

And What About the Men?

While our visible cue theory of representation places the onus on awareness, we do not believe that all citizens will be equally impacted. We believe that the effects of increased female descriptive representation may be conditioned by gender. There has been disagreement within the literature regarding whether the symbolic effects of more women in elected office will be equally felt by women and men. Although scholars have found that greater numbers of female representatives positively affect symbolic representation for men and women (Atkeson and Carrillo 2007), generate more positive views about the democratic process for men and women (Karp and Banducci 2008), and inspire more confidence in legislatures among both men and women (Schwindt-Bayer and Mishler 2005), others found no effects for men due to greater numbers of women in office (Barnes and Burchard 2013) or for men when they are represented by a woman (High-Pippert and Comer 1998: 63).

We expect that women will experience greater change than men in their connection to politics following large jumps in women's election to office. We do not expect that men will be impacted in the same way by enhanced numbers of women in office. This is not because we expect that men will have less awareness of these changes—that somehow men are blinded to the escalating presence of female politicians—but rather because this cue does not resonate with men in the same way that it does for women.[19]

As Mansbridge has explained, the incorporation of a previously excluded group—in this case, women—creates "a social meaning of ability to rule for members of a group in historical contexts where that ability has been seriously questioned" (Mansbridge 1999: 628). The cue has a different meaning for women, who are the historically excluded group, than it does for men. We expect that men will be less impacted by visible changes in women's descriptive representation.

Alternatively, the symbol of greater gender equality in the legislature may cue men in an entirely different way. Status discontent theory (Banaszak and Plutzer 1993; Morgan and Buice 2013) would argue that men may be turned off from politics by the greater inclusion of women. The signaling that comes from the greater descriptive representation of women may cue something different for men than for women, potentially creating a backlash effect. We gauge changes in men's and women's connections to the political process in this book, allowing us to evaluate whether men are largely unaffected by visible changes to women's descriptive representation or are instead politically repelled by these changes.

Disrupting Cues, Distorting Messages

As illustrated in Figure 2.1, the visible cue theory puts forth the idea that either descriptive representation and/or gender quotas could affect

---

[19] We know that female citizens are more likely to remember the names of female politicians (Burns, Schlozman, and Verba 2001; Koch 1997). While this has been interpreted to mean that women are more politically interested when there are people like them representing them, we could also assume that this means that women care more than men that there are people like them representing them in office or as candidates.

symbolic representation but only if these are visible. Either the descriptive representation of women or a gender quota can send a cue which signals to women that they too belong, and this activates their engagement and support for politics.

The cues can however be disrupted. For example, skepticism may distort the message that citizens are receiving. If, for example, citizens believe that gender quotas have not been passed due to a commitment to greater gender equality but instead to appease international organizations, we do not expect that there will be positive effects for symbolic representation. Citizens may similarly see a less formidable increase in women's descriptive representation as more indicative of tokenism than of real change, or they may interpret the presence of a single female president as tokenism. Alternatively, citizens may read these cues through the lens of substantive representation: unless women deliver, there may be little in the way of changes to symbolic representation.

Is There Reason to Fear a Backlash?

> Ms. Rousseff said she been called a cow "about 600,000 times," and attributed her downfall partly to misogyny , . . . Mrs. Kirchner of Argentina, who stepped down in 2015 because of term limits, was often called a "yegua," or female horse, a slang term that means whore.
>
> —Londoño 2017: np

> Now, for example, we are experiencing a backlash . . . political harassment is increasing, [female politicians] are suffering more aggressions, social media is full of offensive things against them.
>
> —Laura Chinchilla, former President of Costa Rica, *Vital Voices* panel, Arizona State University, November 5, 2019

Just as women's gains in elected office are neither automatic nor inevitable, so too are the effects of women's inclusion not always positive. Scholars have found resistance and negative effects of greater numbers of women in office for the way individual legislators are treated and for substantive representation (Beckwith and Cowell-Meyers 2007). Importantly, both gender quotas and rising numbers of women in political power may also elicit a backlash among the public, and such a backlash could manifest in decreased political connections.

Some speculate that "quotas can raise resentment among men, who feel left behind, while simultaneously increasing women's empowerment" (Franceschet, Krook, and Piscopo 2012: 230). Clayton 2015 and Burnet 2011, both examining cases in Africa, find negative attitudes associated with gender quotas (but see Footnote 6). Concerns about a possible backlash among men once quotas have been adopted may have been overstated. Simply put, our research contributes to a small but growing body of evidence that citizens are largely unaware of gender quotas. Backlash, of course, also requires visibility.

More concerning perhaps is the prospect of a backlash against women officeholders. Sanbonmatsu 2008 warns of a negative reaction among the public, especially following visible changes. She points out that in the United States, the 1992 "Year of the Woman" was followed by the "Year of the Angry White Male" in 1994, when men's support for the Republican Party rose substantially. A backlash among the public has been found in other regions of the world as well. Comparing the effects of women's gains in elected office across Southeast and East Asia, Liu 2018 finds lower rates of political discussion, voting, campaign activity, and protest among women in the electorate. Although her study does not allow for gauging the visibility of women's descriptive representation, it is entirely plausible that women's gains in descriptive representation contributed to the decline in participation.

Some may be concerned that women's presence in politics might actually lead to depressed political engagement among men. In this vein, Kittilson and Schwindt-Bayer 2012 find evidence that the shrinking gender gap in political engagement across several countries results from men becoming less interested in politics, not necessarily from women becoming more interested. These findings may be part of a global pattern of men's lower political engagement as a result of women's rising political power or an artifact of men's higher levels to begin with. Previous theorizing about status discontent also suggests that women's progress in politics may come with a backlash against women (see Morgan and Buice 2013). And this reaction against women's gains can elicit a negative reaction among both men and women (Banaszak and Plutzer 1993).

A Note on Terminology

While there has been little disagreement in defining both descriptive representation ("who are the representatives?") and substantive representation ("what do these representatives do?"), academics have struggled to articulate a common understanding of symbolic representation. In the process of symbolic representation, a response is elicited among those who are represented. Scholars have used an assortment of approaches to measure the effects of political symbols, including examining political knowledge, political interest, attitudes toward women in politics, attitudes toward government, trust in political institutions, political participation (covering the gamut from signing petitions, to casting a ballot, to running for office), and satisfaction with democracy (Alexander 2012; Wolbrecht and Campbell 2007; Campbell and Wolbrecht 2006; Kittilson 2005; Burns, Schlozman, and Verba 2001; Carroll 1985).

What is a symbol? Symbols inspire emotions. There are different types of symbols. Symbols are typically visual objects (flags and statues) but might also be discursive, such as laws (Lombardo and Meier 2014: 40). "But human beings, too, can be thought of as symbols, can under the right circumstances stand for a nation just as the flag does" (Pitkin 1967: 92). Individuals can serve as symbols, but so too can collective bodies.

Because of the inconsistent and overly broad definitions and ways of measuring symbolic representation within the academic literature, we use the term *political connection* throughout this book as we gauge the effects of symbols. By political connections we refer not only to political engagement (i.e., the "psychological orientations towards politics" that citizens hold (Burns, Schlozman, and Verba 2001: 335) but also to political support, which includes political trust (in a variety of government institutions) and satisfaction with the functioning of democracy.

Saward urges scholars to focus on "understanding what representation does rather than what it is; to explore the effects of its invocation rather than its institutional embodiment; to stress its dynamic character rather than its correctly understood forms or types" (2010: 4). From this, we take care to conceive of representation as a dynamic process and are concerned with its effects over time. Our approach to investigating this dynamic process is to empirically analyze a wide array of plausible responses to changes in political symbols.

Conclusion

Having established how visibility matters to the dynamics of representation, the chapters that follow will empirically examine the dynamic relationships between gender quotas, descriptive representation, and symbolic representation. We first turn our attention to these relationships comparatively by looking at a select group of Latin American countries. Based on our interpretation of representation as a process, in each case we are concerned only with changes over time within one country and not on cross-national comparisons. We then focus on a unique election in Uruguay. The analytical leverage afforded us by the Uruguayan case allows us to analyze this relationship in depth to determine whether increased descriptive representation does yield gains for symbolic representation.

CHAPTER 3 | Women's Political Inclusion
in Latin America: The Challenges
of Gauging Visibility

[The legal changes] have opened up a series of opportunities and
circumstances that allow women's participation, and they have
changed the political scene and the social imagination. Girls,
adolescents, and young women can aspire to a political position and
political participation in the future.

—Marcia Ramírez, Nicaragua's Minister of Family (Álvarez 2017)

WHAT HAPPENS WHEN women's political representation doubles overnight? The previous chapter presented an analytical framework depicting
how women's numbers in office can act as a symbol to elicit greater connection to the political process. Importantly, we noted these gains in
women's presence must be visible to ordinary citizens. Sizable gains in
women's descriptive representation may have more noticeable effects on
the connections between citizens and the democratic process than incremental growth. In this chapter, we therefore turn to looking at such sizable
gains or "big jumps" in women's legislative representation across Latin
America.

In Latin America, notable increases in women's representation in political office have regularly been the result of gender quota legislation.
All Latin American countries save Guatemala have implemented gender
quotas. Yet, the adoption of gender quotas is not in itself sufficient to en-
sure their success. Academics have identified a number of practices that
make quotas more or less effective (Htun and Jones 2002; Jones 2004;
Matland and Taylor 1997). In addition, scholars have found that initial

Seeing Women, Strengthening Democracy. Magda Hinojosa and Miki Caul Kittilson, Oxford University Press (2020).
© Oxford University Press. DOI: 10.1093/oso/9780197526941.001.0001.

quotas are often rife with loopholes that must be addressed through further legislation or via other means (Araújo and García 2006; Hinojosa and Piscopo 2013). Throughout Latin America, we have seen that quotas have been revised repeatedly both to close loopholes and to raise their thresholds. Quota thresholds originally set at 30 percent have been pushed up to 40 percent or to parity.

But even when gender quotas work well, we rarely see enormous increases in women's representation from one election to the next. In Chapter 1, Figure 1.2 provides data at two points in time, 20 years apart. While we have seen incredible changes to women's representation in some Latin American countries across time, we very rarely see big swings in the number of women in office from one election to the next.

Yet, there have been instances of women's parliamentary representation doubling from one election to the next in countries as diverse as Albania and Zimbabwe. In examining women's representation since 1997, we see this doubling of women's numbers in lower houses or unicameral legislatures in more than 85 countries, with some of these countries seeing multiple leaps in women's representation.[1] For example, in Argentina's lower house, women's representation increased by at least 200 percent on four different occasions, without ever rising above nine percent. If we also examine upper houses of parliament, we find leaps of this type in women's representation in 31 countries from across the globe, all of which saw a doubling of women's representation from one election to the next. An example would be Argentina's Senate, where women's representation doubled to nearly 6 percent in 1995 and then dramatically rose to 33 percent in the following elections.

We define a big jump as women's numbers in the legislature doubling from one election to the next to land above 20 percent. This allows us to exclude instances—as in the Argentine Senate where the percentage of women grew from 3 percent to 6 percent—where there are notable

---

[1] Albania, Algeria, Andorra, Angola, Antigua and Barbuda, Bahrain, Bangladesh, Belarus, Belize, Bhutan, Bolivia, Bosnia and Herzegovina, Botswana, Bulgaria, Burundi, Cambodia, Cameroon, Chad, Comoros, Congo, Croatia, Djibouti, Dominica, Ecuador, Egypt, Equatorial Guinea, Ethiopia, Fiji, Gambia, Grenada, Guinea, Haiti, Honduras, Iraq, Jordan, Kenya, Kiribati, Kuwait, Kyrgyzstan, Laos, Lebanon, Lesotho, Liberia, Liechtenstein, Lithuania, Macedonia, Madagascar, Maldives, Mali, Marshall Islands, Mauritania, Mauritius, Monaco, Mongolia, Morocco, Nauru, Nepal, Nicaragua, Niger, Oman, Pakistan, Palau, Panama, Papua New Guinea, Paraguay, Saint Kitts and Nevis, Saint Lucia, Saint Vincent and the Grenadines, Samoa, Sao Tome and Principe, Saudi Arabia, Slovenia, Solomon Islands, Somalia, South Korea, Suriname, Swaziland, Tajikistan, Togo, Tonga, Turkey, Tuvalu, Ukraine, United Arab Emirates, Uzbekistan, Vanuatu, Venezuela, and Zimbabwe have all seen their percentages of women in their lower or single houses of parliament double.

TABLE 3.1 Big Jumps in Women's Legislative Representation

COUNTRY	CHANGE IN WOMEN'S REPRESENTATION	DATE OF ELECTION	DATE OF PRE-ELECTION LAPOP SURVEY	DATE OF POST-ELECTION LAPOP SURVEY
Honduras	5% → 23%	November 27, 2005	February–March 2004	June–July 2006
Bolivia	3% → 47%	December 6, 2009	February–March 2008	February–March 2010
Nicaragua	21% → 40%	November 6, 2011	January–February 2010	February–March 2012
Panama	8% → 19%	May 4, 2014	January–March 2012	March–May 2017
Bolivia	25% → 53%	October 12, 2014	March–May 2014	March–May 2017

increases but where women remain very poorly represented. Since 2000, and excluding Uruguay, which we detail in subsequent chapters, we have seen seven big jumps in Latin America.

We list the instances that we will investigate in Table 3.1.[2] The table lists the country where we saw each of these big jumps, the date of the election that marked a dramatic change in women's legislative representation, and dates of pre- and post-election surveys. We refer to these as pre- and post-election surveys because these are the most temporally proximate LAPOP surveys that correspond to the time periods before and after the election of interest. These surveys, however, were not intended as either pre- or post-election surveys; indeed, Carlin, Singer, and Zechmeister note that the LAPOP surveys are "not designed as an election survey" (Carlin et al. 2015: 18).

As the data in Table 3.1 demonstrate, the timing of surveys rarely aligns well for the purpose of comparing political engagement and political support before and after elections.[3] For example, in Bolivia the 2014 elections led to a sizable change in the gender composition of Bolivia's lower house.

---

[2] To increase the number of cases that we consider, we (1) consider a doubling to have occurred in Nicaragua when women's representation increased from 20.6 percent to 40.2 percent; and (2) include Panama, although the final percentage of women was short of the 20 percent cutoff (19%). We also exclude two cases of big jumps due to an absence of available data from LAPOP for these early time periods. The first is from the Argentine Senate. Women's representation jumped from 6 percent to 33 percent following the 2001 elections, which were the first elections in which senators were directly elected. The second case is from Nicaragua, where women's representation in the unicameral legislature doubled from 10 percent to 20 percent after the 2001 elections.

[3] The Panamanian election took place on May 4, 2014. Because the 2014 LAPOP survey was carried out between March 13 and May 3, we opted to instead use the 2012 data. This close to the election, the full list of candidates would have been announced and it is possible that the public would have had a very good idea of who could be elected. Data on LAPOP fieldwork dates are

But the most temporally proximate survey does not occur until March 2017, more than two years after those election results. The same is true of Panama. In order to assess the effects of large changes to the descriptive representation of women, we would ideally see surveys in the field close to the election date. Levels of political engagement and support vary considerably based on proximity to election, as campaigns and news coverage make politics more salient. After those elected take office, they may (or may not) engage in intentional acts of substantive representation, including speaking in the legislature, promoting legislation, and voting on bills. The further from the election, the greater the cumulative effect of this confounding substantive representation. Because our focus here is on descriptive representation, we desire surveys close to the election dates.

In the sections that follow, we examine each of these cases in turn (but group the two Bolivian cases together). Taken together, our in-depth examination of these instances of sizable jumps in this chapter reveals that available survey data is inadequate for answering the types of questions we are asking. These surveys are simply not timed to capture election effects. The fact that the pre- and post-election surveys come long before or long after the election of interest is especially problematic in countries, like many of those in Latin America, where we see tremendous political change in very short periods of time. In this chapter our analysis of a few select cases in Latin America makes clear that absent intense fieldwork, there is no way to assess whether changes to women's descriptive representation were visible; if these changes have not been seen, they will not be felt. In addition, we find that for the countries that we study, too much changes in too little time to be able to isolate the effects of jumps in descriptive representation.

Big Jumps in Women's Political Representation in Honduras

Women received the right to vote in Honduras in 1954. Women's representation in congress had barely nudged since the 1980s, until the introduction of the gender quota. Women had held 2.4 percent of seats in 1981, 6.7 percent in 1985, and 9.4 percent in 1989. Until 2005, women's share of legislative seats never surpassed 9.4 percent (Espinosa 2011: 46).

available here: https://www.vanderbilt.edu/lapop/ab2016/Fieldwork_dates_tables_2004-2016_17_092517.pdf.

The country's first female presidential candidate ran in 1997, and al-though she lost, she received 43 percent of the vote, as indicated in Table 1.1 in Chapter 1. Honduras would once again have a viable female presidential candidate in 2013, when Xiomara Castro de Zelaya, wife of the former president, ran for office and obtained 29 percent of the vote. A third woman ran for the presidency in 2017 but was not considered vi-able (Sierra 2018: 189). Women have also obtained more significant rep-resentation in ministerial positions in recent years. While in 1998–2001, women held 27.8 percent of ministerial posts, these were in important ministries. Women's ministerial representation dropped in 2002–2005 to 16.7 percent but surged again in 2006–2010, when women held one-third of ministerial positions (Espinosa 2011). Figure 1.1 in Chapter 1 displays this growth in women's share of cabinet seats from 1999–2014. Women have also had representation in the judicial branch. Women held more than half of judicial appointments to the Supreme Court of Justice during the time period from 2002–2009 (8 of 15 positions), but their representation had dropped to only one-third of the justices on the Supreme Court of Justice the following decade (Taylor-Robinson 2009; Sierra 2018).

Women's legislative representation was largely stagnant until the use of gender quotas.[4] Women held only 6.7 percent of seats in 1985; 15 years later, women held only 7.4 percent of legislative seats (Ferreira Rubio 2013). The significant change occurred in 2005 with the election of a leg-islative body that was one-quarter female. In the elections that followed, women's legislative representation dropped to 19.5 percent. Ferreira Rubio 2013 argues that the decrease in female legislators in 2009 is the result of the coup against Zelaya, which led many candidates to resign their candidacies over concerns about transparency and to protest the coup itself. While women's representation increased to 25.8 percent with the 2013 elections, it dropped after the 2017 election despite the fact that parity rules now applied (Sierra 2018).

Honduras adopted a weak gender quota in 2000, which included an initial threshold of 20 percent that would be increased over time, but lacked sanctions for noncompliance. As part of broader electoral reforms, the gender quota was revised in 2004. While the new quota in-cluded a 30 percent threshold, it no longer called for progressively higher thresholds, and the quota ended up "functioning more as a ceiling" than as a floor for women's legislative candidacies (Sierra 2018: 193). Parties

---

[4] The first elections under quota laws actually saw a nominal decrease in women's representation, due to lack of compliance by political parties (Ferreira Rubio 2013).

routinely failed to meet their quota obligations. For example, for the 2009 elections nearly one of every five lists put forth by the *Partido Nacional* failed to meet the quota, as did a whopping 32 percent of the lists of the *Partido Liberal* (Taylor-Robinson 2009: 475). The law would not be revised again until 2012, when a new threshold of 40 percent was set (Sierra 2018). A revised version of the law called for parity. But even with parity provisions in place, women's representation did not increase dramatically, rising only to 21 percent. The gender quota has largely been viewed as "weak and inefficient"; Freidenberg explains that the law has been limited due to three factors. First, parity regulations are applied to pre-candidates for primary elections and not to candidacies for the general elections. Second, the law does not require alternation of gender on party lists. Finally, Honduras uses an open-list system, which means that voters ultimately decide among a party's candidates (Freidenberg 2019: 3).

Honduras' unicameral assembly saw women's representation increase from 5 percent to 23 percent after the 2005 elections. Yet, as displayed in Figure 1.5 in the 2004–2019 period, LAPOP surveys show a statistically significant gender gap in political interest in Honduras. Among Honduran women, 27.4 percent report some or a lot of political interest, while nearly 32 percent of Honduran men report some or a lot of political interest. Taken together, we find little evidence in the LAPOP surveys of any disappearance of the gender gap in political interest or democratic satisfaction.

As in other countries, we are incapable of assessing whether this change in women's descriptive representation—a jump from 5 percent female representation in congress to 23 percent—was visible to everyday Hondurans. Women's share of ministerial positions had also surged between the pre-election and post-election survey (Espinosa 2011); here too we had seen women's representation double as a result of the election. Additionally, the legislative candidate that received the most votes in 2005 was a woman (Taylor-Robinson 2009: 478). The 2005 elections were not just notable because of their effects on women's descriptive representation; these elections also marked the first time in 70 years that Afro-Hondurans obtained representation in the National Assembly. Four Afro-Hondurans were elected to the legislative body (Taylor-Robinson 2009).

Several simultaneous political events could reduce the visibility of this sizable increase in women's election to the legislature. This time period in Honduran history is notable for an increase in crime and violence, and greater uncertainty for the general population. Additionally, there were significant changes to the political system.[5] The 2005 election was the first to utilize open-list proportional representation, rather than the closed-list system that had previously been employed, and the first time that primaries were used to select candidates for deputy lists (Taylor-Robinson 2009). These changes dramatically altered the composition of the legislative body by reducing reelection, and could have changed people's connections to politics as new faces and new parties gained power for the first time. Moreover, the 2005 elections were the first in which Hondurans would elect a single vice-president. The 2005 elections moved the presidency out of the hands of the National Party and into the hands of the Liberal Party, and also gave a plurality of seats to the Liberal Party. Additionally, the 2005 campaign itself could have resulted in changes to citizens' political connections. Zelaya had campaigned on a promise to provide more social programs and to root out corruption. These would include raising the minimum wage, free primary schooling, free electricity for the poorest, mass literacy campaigns, and subsidizing gas.

Big Jumps in Women's Political Representation in Bolivia

Bolivian women obtained the right to vote in 1952, and although the country had an interim female president at the end of the 1970s, it did not stand out in Latin America for its female representation until recently. Today, Bolivia distinguishes itself due to its inclusion of women in politics.

Women's representation in the Bolivian legislature had been boosted by the adoption of a gender quota in 1997. As one feminist activist explained, obtaining a gender quota "was not a concession, and it wasn't a gift from the male deputies or from the Legislative Assembly. Instead it was something that we'd been working on, something that the women's organizations had been demanding as part of a very interesting and untold alliance with female political party militants" (Choque Aldana 2013: 129). The quota, which called for a 30 percent threshold, had a discernible effect[6] on the percentage of female candidates and officeholders, but it was the adoption of gender parity that would push Bolivia to have some of the highest

---

[5] The coup that overthrew Honduran president Manuel Zelaya in June 2009 occurred prior to the post-election survey, but President Zelaya was in office during this survey wave.
[6] A number of efforts to cheat the quota have been documented (see Hinojosa 2012), such as registering male candidates under female names (i.e., Juan as Juana). Because of this, a number of civil society organizations worked together to launch a campaign known as *Listas para las Listas* (a play on words that translates as Ready for the Lists) to keep a watchful eye that party lists were complying with quota requirements in the 2009 elections (Choque Aldana 2014: 350).

levels of women's legislative representation in the world. The move to parity was inspired by traditional indigenous ideas about gender complementarity; according to Ewig, "their concept of gender relations, rooted in *chachawarmi*, led them to view 50-50 gender parity as the only proposal that would reflect their vision of gender relations" (Ewig 2018: 450).[7]

The extraordinary increase in women's representation in Bolivia's legislative bodies is all the more startling given the fairly minimal presence that women had in Bolivia previously. From the early 1990s to 2001, women's representation in the Chamber of Deputies hovered around 10 percent. It is only in 2002 that we begin to see more significant progress, which culminates in a big leap following the 2014 elections (Archenti and Tula 2014). Women's representation in the Senate was routinely under 4 percent until the 2009 elections, which saw the percentage of women catapulted from 3.7 percent to 44.4 percent.[8] Moreover, women also entered leadership positions within these legislative bodies. By 2014, women simultaneously presided over the two chambers of the legislature, with Gabriela Montaño and Rebeca Delgado heading up the Senate and Chamber of Deputies, respectively. However, Bolivia is one of the few countries in Latin America that has not yet witnessed the candidacy of a viable female contender for the presidency.

Women's representation in other powerful bodies also received significant boosts. In 2010, Bolivian President Evo Morales announced: "My great dream has come true: half of the members of my cabinet are women, and half are men" (Chávez 2010). Morales' first cabinet had half as many women as his second historic cabinet.[9] Women also made significant inroads into the judicial branch. By 2012, women occupied 33.3 percent of seats in the Supreme Tribunal of Justice, 57.1 percent of seats in the Constitutional Tribunal, and 42.9 percent of seats in the Supreme Electoral Tribunal (Choque Aldana 2014: 337). Despite the advances in women's presence in politics, Bolivian women politicians have been plagued by acts of hostility and violence—especially at the local level—that undermine and deter their political participation (Choque Aldana 2014; Restrepo Sanín 2016).

---

[7] Ewig argues that the adoption of parity "is perhaps the most robust example to date in Bolivia of political intersectionality leading to reconceived intersectional interests" (Ewig 2018: 448–449).
[8] The exception to this pattern was the time period from 2002–2005, when women comprised slightly less than 15 percent of all senators.
[9] Of this historic cabinet, one female minister, Nardi Suxo, noted: "there's effective participation [by women]. The opinions of the female ministers . . . they are taken into account by the president" (Choque Aldana 2013: 154).

In Bolivia, women's representation doubled on two occasions. First, women's representation increased dramatically in the Bolivian senate following the 2009 elections, climbing from just 3 percent to 47 percent. Second, women's representation in the lower house of congress increased from 25 percent to 53 percent following the 2014 elections. Yet isolating the impact of these gains for mass-level political engagement and support is tenuous using existing survey data. Specifically, the timing of the surveys may obscure the effects of women's record gains. The LAPOP survey for 2014 was gathered prior to the election: the election took place on October 12, 2014, and the LAPOP surveys were conducted between March 26 and May 18 of that year. The next survey wave comes in 2016, which is two years after the big gains.

Despite big jumps in women's election to office, female citizens remain less politically interested and less supportive of democracy. The merged data presented in Figure 1.5 of Chapter 1 reveals that 31.2 percent of Bolivian men report some or a lot of political interest, as compared with the 22.6 percent of women who report the same levels of interest. And a more fine-grained analysis of the same LAPOP surveys in 2014 and 2016 show that the gender differences remain statistically significant at those time points.

Were citizens aware of the significant changes to women's descriptive representation following the 2009 and 2014 elections? Unfortunately, we are unable to assess whether Bolivians noticed the sizable boost to women's legislative representation. Women's visibility may have been amplified due to Morales' historic parity cabinet, which he appointed in 2010. Not only had the elections since 2005 brought more and more women into office, they had also led to the descriptive representation of the indigenous, who had traditionally been excluded from politics. President Morales had appointed three indigenous women to his cabinet in 2010. By the 2014 elections, indigenous women held 19 percent of seats in congress; a decade earlier, indigenous women had no descriptive representatives (Rousseau and Ewig 2017). Archenti and Tula argue that the use of parity "highlighted women's participation" as well as participation by the indigenous (Archenti and Tula 2014: 61).

Moreover, there were other concurrent political events taking place that could affect both men's and women's orientations toward the political process, which could be captured by the 2008 and 2010 LAPOP surveys. August 2008 saw an unsuccessful recall referendum on President Morales, followed by anti-government protests. Bolivian relations with the United States soured, leading not only to the expulsion of the US ambassador but also to the cessation of US Drug Enforcement Agency operations in the country. More importantly, in January 2009, voters approved a new constitution lauded for its embrace of indigenous rights (Rousseau and Ewig 2017). The 2009 elections did not just mark a jump in women's representation; they also marked the reelection of Evo Morales, the country's first indigenous president and a source of tremendous pride for Bolivia's majority indigenous population.[10] These elections too brought other indigenous people—including women—into office both via elected and appointed positions.

Similarly, before and after the 2014 big jump in women's numbers in elected office, several important political events may confound the effects of women's inclusion. On the heels of a natural disaster, Morales won a third term in office in October 2014. Yet, a referendum to reform the constitution to allow Morales to seek reelection failed. The referendum may have dampened the visibility of women's gains in the eyes of the electorate focusing attention instead on Morales' desire to stay in the presidency for an indefinite period of time.

Big Jumps in Women's Political Representation in Nicaragua

The story of women's political representation in Nicaragua is closely tied to the *Frente Sandinista de Liberación Nacional* (FSLN) and the Nicaraguan revolution. While Nicaraguan women acquired suffrage in 1955 and the first woman entered the legislative body in 1957, it was the revolution and the revolutionary party that opened doors to women's representation (see Kampwirth 2010). The FSLN had integrated women since its beginning in 1961 and during the revolutionary period (1979–1990) women held important political positions as ambassadors and ministers, increased their representation in the legislature to 13.5 percent in 1984, and constituted half the police force (Hinojosa and Vijil Gurdián 2012: 63). Moreover, "state mobilization of women in the Nicaraguan revolutionary period was fundamental to the development of a strong autonomous feminist movement in the post-Sandinista period"[11] (Ewig 1999: 79). Although women made

---

[10] The election of Evo Morales had tremendous symbolic effects on Bolivia's indigenous population. Ewig notes that the election of Morales even changed her own fieldwork experiences, as Morales' election "meant that indigenous women felt empowered to speak to me (a white U.S. researcher) frankly, in ways that may not have occurred at a different time" (Ewig 2018: 435).
[11] Ewig 1999 notes that the Sandinista's record on women's issues was nonetheless "mixed" and that a number of important issues, including abortion and divorce, were left largely unaddressed.

sizable gains, it was the defeat of the Sandinistas in 1990 that ushered in the country's first female president.

As Table 1.1 in Chapter 1 shows, Nicaragua was the first country in Latin America to have a woman as a viable presidential candidate. Violeta Chamorro was seen as a political widow[12] "who could garner widespread support and serve as a reconciliatory force; after all, as she often mentioned, of her four children, two were Sandinistas and two were Contras. If she could keep her family united, she could do the same for the nation" (Hinojosa 2012: 124). Her presidency (1990–1996) signaled a more conservative turn for the nation and a drop in women's political representation. Further, since that time there have been no other viable female presidential candidates.

The election of President Daniel Ortega launched a period of tremendous growth in women's political representation. He had announced during his 2007 campaign that he would appoint a cabinet comprised equally of men and women. Figure 1.1 in Chapter 1 shows that the percentage of women among the presidential cabinet soared after Ortega came into office, reaching over 45 percent by 2014. The FSLN, the president's party, had maintained a more gender equitable stance and had adopted its own voluntary gender quotas in 1996, which it fortified in advance of the 2011 elections. The big jump in women's representation that comes in 2011 occurs without a national gender quota, but is instead a result of the FSLN's own internal efforts to increase women's presence in the legislature by presenting parity candidate lists (Samqui 2016). The FSLN's parity lists led to significant changes to women's officeholding in Nicaragua due to the party's electoral dominance. Women won over 40 percent of seats in the 2011 elections (Archenti and Tula 2014: 53). Women's representation in the legislature was further amplified once a national parity regulation was put into place: women obtained 45.7 percent of seats as a result of the 2016 elections.

Nicaragua's big jump in women's representation then comes after the 2011 elections, when women's representation in the unicameral legislature jumped from 20.6 percent to 40.2 percent. Yet, Figure 1.5 in Chapter 1 demonstrates that over the period from 2004–2019 a statistically significant

---

As Saint-Germain and Chávez Metoyer explain, "women were often asked to put gender-related issues and concerns on hold" (2008: 70).

[12] Technically, Chamorro was not a political widow, as her late husband never held political office. For more information, see Hinojosa 2012.

gender gap in political interest existed in Nicaragua. Nearly 32 percent of men report some or more political interest, while slightly less than 25 percent of women report the same.

The confluence of salient political events and the timing of existing surveys may mask the effects of these big jumps. Although a LAPOP survey was fielded a few months after the election, the previous survey took place approximately 24 months prior to the election in January and February of 2010. The timing is far from ideal for examining election effects, especially given the tremendous changes that were taking place in Nicaragua during this time period.

Further complicating analysis of trends over time in Nicaragua, we cannot assess whether the changes in women's descriptive representation were widely seen by Nicaraguan citizens. Citizens may have noticed these changes or the increases in the numbers of women in cabinet (as demonstrated in Figure 1.1 in Chapter 1), but other contemporaneous changes may have sent different signals about women's equality as citizens. The most notable woman in politics might have been the president's wife, Rosario Murillo. While it was only in 2016 that she took on the vice-presidency, Murillo had already been given extensive powers by her husband. Citizens too may have noticed that Ortega had taken a more conservative approach since returning to office, talking about his Catholic faith and drastically curtailing abortion access in 2006.

Finally, we certainly do not expect that women's representation is the only—or the most important—factor that influences citizens' political connections. During this period of time, Nicaragua underwent some significant changes that could affect citizens' connections to the political process. Daniel Ortega, who had led the Nicaraguan revolution, had returned to the presidency in 2007 and appeared to embrace authoritarianism. The 2011 elections may have doubled women's representation in the National Assembly, but they were controversial because President Ortega had been allowed to run for reelection. During the latter part of 2009, the Constitutional Court lifted the ban on presidential reelection, allowing Ortega to run for and win the elections in November 2011. Ortega increasingly moved toward authoritarianism by disqualifying other political parties from participating in elections and preventing international observers from watching municipal elections in 2008 and national elections in 2011. Numerous allegations of voter fraud also surfaced against the government.

Big Jumps in Women's Political Representation in Panama

In Panama, women gained suffrage in 1946. Although women's political presence was less common in Panama than it had been in Nicaragua, the notable exception was the election of Mireya Moscoso to the presidency in 1999, as noted in Table 1.1 in Chapter 1. Her rise to power "most closely approximates that of the stereotypical political widow" (Hinojosa 2012: 124). Moscoso's husband had served as president of Panama on three separate occasions, and Moscoso only entered politics after her husband's death and under the banner of his political party. Moscoso first ran for the presidency (unsuccessfully) in 1994 and then won the 1999 election.

Despite having a woman at the political helm, in most ways Panamanian women lagged behind others during this same time period. Women gained only 8 percent of legislative seats in 1994 and only 10 percent in 1999. Fifteen years later, women had not made progress, holding only 8 percent of seats prior to the 2014 elections. Women's participation as cabinet ministers was also low, 14 percent in 2014–2015, and 21 percent in 2015–2016; at the highest levels of the judiciary, there are nine posts; only one was occupied by a woman during the 2014–2016 period (INAMU 2017). Further, the presidential bid of the second woman in Panama to run for this office, Balbina Herrera, was unsuccessful in 2009 (see Table 1.1 in Chapter 1).

The adoption of gender quota laws across Latin American countries followed international pressure fermented at the United Nations Fourth World Conference on Women in Beijing in 1995. Panama was one of the countries that ceded to this pressure early, adopting a gender quota in 1997. Yet these quotas have largely been seen as a failure. Although the original quota legislation included a 30 percent threshold, women's representation averaged 11 percent in the years following the quota (Gray 2015). The Panamanian quota has been ineffective in part because it is applied not to candidate lists but to party primary lists, although this is not the only weakness of this legislation. The quota initially could be applied to alternate positions rather than to titleholder (sometimes referred to as principle) positions; according to Gray, "parties have even fulfilled the 30 percent quota without actually nominating any women to run as principle candidates for Deputy" (Gray 2015: 296). The generous exemption clause and lack of sanctions for noncompliance meant that the quota law was largely ignored. The law was revamped in 2012, increasing the threshold to 50 percent but maintaining the exemption clause, which allowed parties to avoid sanctions if they could not find enough female candidates to meet the quota (Gray 2015). The newly revised law had little effect: for the 2014 election, none of the political parties came close to parity in their candidacies. The party with the largest share of female candidates (*Partido Popular*) included women as 20.9 percent of candidates (Parra Badilla, Pérez Meneses, and Sáenz Leandro 2015).

The first election after the application of the quota proved the limits of the quota law, as the number of female deputies failed to increase. Women held just under 10 percent of seats (and had held 8 percent in the previous congress). After the 2004 elections, women's representation increased to 15 percent, but their representation decreased after the 2009 elections when women held only six of the 71 seats in the National Assembly (Gray 2015). Women's representation increased in 2014 "despite the weak quota rather than because of it" (Gray 2015: 298). Gray attributes the rise in women's descriptive representation following the 2014 elections to incumbency advantages rather than to the quota. Since the implementation of the first quota law, the percentage of female candidates has continued to be quite low.

Although Panama's legislature saw women's representation double from 8 percent to 19 percent following the 2014 elections, the data from LAPOP surveys carried out between 2012–2017 yield gender gaps in political interest that are characterized by an ebb and flow rather than any clear patterns. In short, the gender gap in political interest in Panama persists over time. Supporting this finding of persistent gaps, Figure 1.5 in Chapter 1 shows that gender differences in political interest were statistically significant in Panama. For democratic satisfaction, gender differences are minimal—both before and after the sizable gains in elected office.

A clear test of the effects of these sizable gains proves difficult. The timing of surveys is insufficient to measure these effects. The 2014 LAPOP surveys took place between March 13 and May 3, and elections took place the following day on May 4. The next survey comes more than two years after the elections and is likely to capture changing attitudes toward a range of events that occurred in the intervening years, and not just attitudes about the election.

We are unable to assess—as we will do for Uruguay—the level of visibility of these changes to women's legislative representation. Women's representation in congress more than doubled as a result of the 2014 elections, but we cannot know whether ordinary Panamanian citizens were aware of this. Panamanians may have noted that 2014 also ushered in the country's first female vice-president: Isabel Saint Malo de Alvarado of the *Partido Panameñista*. Or, they may have noticed that most political parties had opted to run a female vice-presidential candidate alongside the male presidential candidate in the 2014 elections (Acuña de Molina 2018). We do have indications that the quota law itself had garnered little visibility. In a nationally representative survey of 700 Panamanian citizens carried out in 2007, a full ten years after the quota had first been adopted, only 18 percent expressed familiarity with the quota law (Diagnóstico 2007: 50).[13]

Moreover, during the time period between the pre-election survey (2012) and the post-election survey (2017), we have significant political activity in Panama that could lead to changes in citizens' political engagement and support. The time period of analysis for Panama is complicated by significant protests (October 2012), amnesty being given to criminal gangs (July 2014), corruption charges against the previous president (January 2015), and international attention over the use of Panama as a tax haven (April 2016). While the sitting vice-president won the 2014 elections, he had become a critic of his predecessor, who would be charged with corruption the following year.

Conclusion

Close examination of the timing of these sizable gains in women's numbers in elected office reveals that publicly available survey data are often inadequate for properly investigating the questions that we seek to examine. It is important for us to keep in mind that while LAPOP surveys are first-rate in their quality, their timing is not designed to capture or isolate the effects of the election for citizen attitudes. After the election, men and women legislators alike engage in intentional acts of representation. This substantive representation may impact the public's orientations toward the political process, depending of course on the visibility of those policy efforts. The timing of surveys for each of these countries makes it impossible to avoid conflating the effects of descriptive versus substantive representation. To answer the kinds of questions that we have, we ideally want to see surveys occurring both shortly before and shortly after an election.

In each case examined in depth in this chapter, women's gains in the legislature were sizable. But, were they visible? Only in-depth analysis of each of these cases would allow us any confidence to say whether these

---

[13] We believe that the survey overstates the percentage of Panamanians actually familiar with the quota law. As we discuss in the chapter that follows, question wording is important. The question asked in this survey was: "Did you know that in Panama there is a law establishing that 30 percent of candidates must be women?"

changes to descriptive representation were noticed by citizens. The lack of clear patterns in political engagement and support revealed in this chapter may be due to limited visibility of women's descriptive representation in these countries.

The timing of the existing survey waves renders the data simply inadequate to test our questions with much precision. Each of these cases demands that we consider other potentially confounding social and political changes that were taking place in these countries during these same periods of time. Could it be that the changes in political interest in Nicaragua are driven not by increases in women's descriptive representation but instead by the election and policies of Daniel Ortega? Could the removal of the ban on presidential reelection in 2009, which was widely seen as a way to perpetuate Ortega in power, change citizens' political interest? Significant changes to the Nicaraguan constitution also occurred during this same time period. Could these have affected citizens' engagement with politics?

This chapter makes clear that in order to understand how women's descriptive representation can affect citizen engagement with politics we must examine in-country changes over time. As Kittilson and Schwindt-Bayer succinctly state, "What some scholars have attributed to the effects of women's presence in office may in fact be a result of some other related, but distinct, outcome of electoral institutions or the institutions themselves" (2012: 23).

For that reason, we turn our attention in the chapters that follow to Uruguay, where our in-depth analysis allows us confidence that the changes that we see are not due to other electoral institutions or political changes. Chapter 4 describes the Uruguayan context and the sizable jump in women's election to office and, importantly, gauges visibility. As we noted in the previous chapter, symbols can only evoke attitudinal changes when they are observed.

CHAPTER 4 | Invisible Laws, Visible Gains
Gender and Politics in Uruguay

I think we are more visible today. There are more of us in the Senate
now. It just becomes so obvious.

—Interview with Senator Daniela Payssé, June 10, 2015

NEITHER THE ADOPTION of gender quotas nor a dramatic increase in
women's descriptive representation will affect everyday citizens if they
are unaware of these changes, as we explained in Chapter 2. This chapter
therefore examines the Uruguayan case in detail to determine if either the
quota or women's greater presence in politics were visible to citizens. Did
ordinary Uruguayans know of the gender quota? Were the changes to the
composition of the Senate obvious to them, as Senator Payssé indicated?

First, we discuss the underrepresentation of women in politics in
Uruguay, which led to demands for a gender quota. We then direct our
attention to examining the visibility of the gender quota, before turning to
our analysis of the visibility that changes to women's descriptive representation received. Our understanding of these processes is enmeshed in the
deeper context of Uruguayan politics.

Women's Historic Underrepresentation in Politics: From
Slow Gains to Big Jumps

The descriptive representation of women has historically been low in
Uruguay—lagging behind much of Latin America—and rising only slowly

Seeing Women, Strengthening Democracy. Magda Hinojosa and Miki Caul Kittilson, Oxford University Press (2020).
© Oxford University Press. DOI: 10.1093/oso/9780197526941.001.0001.

since the return to democracy in 1984. Uruguayan women were largely absent from the executive, legislative, and judicial branches of power.

In the founding elections after the return to democracy, women obtained no representation in the parliament.[1] Over the course of the next 15 years, women never occupied more than two seats in the upper chamber or more than seven seats in the lower chamber. Women finally surpassed the 10 percent mark in the lower house in 1999 (but were still shy of obtaining that 10 percent in the Senate). But a full decade later, women's representation in the legislature had barely budged: women held just 12.1 percent of seats in the Chamber of Representatives and 12.9 percent of seats in the Senate (IPU 2019).

Women's gains were similarly hobbled across the branches of government. Women's participation in the executive branch had long been meager. Not only had no woman served as either president or vice-president,[2] but women had also been underrepresented in cabinet ministries. In 2014, one of every four cabinet posts in Latin America was occupied by a woman (Htun and Piscopo 2014), but in Uruguay only 12.5 percent of cabinet ministers were women. The highest court in the land, known as the *Suprema Corte de Justicia*, had seen a total of three women justices prior to 2010.[3] At the subnational level, women have been routinely absent from executive power. The country is divided into 19 administrative units; of the 19 intendants (a position that is similar to serving as governor), 18 were men in 2014.

Women's underrepresentation in politics led to efforts to adopt gender quotas. While early efforts began in the late 1980s (see Archenti and Johnson 2006), it was only in 2009 that Uruguayan feminists succeeded in getting a quota law passed (Johnson and Moreni 2009). The gender quota upended this pattern of glacially paced growth.

The gender quota law, Law #18,476, states that "candidates of both sexes must be represented in every three places on electoral lists, either throughout the entire list or in the first 15 places. Where only two seats are contested, one of the two candidates must be a woman." The law specifically prevented parties from pooling female candidates at the bottom of their lists and disallowed the use of political alternate positions as a means

---

[1] Uruguayans refer to their congress as the parliament. In keeping with their vernacular, we also refer to their legislative body as the parliament.

[2] Lucía Topolansky became the nation's first female vice-president after the second wave of our survey, when the previous vice-president resigned his post in 2017.

[3] Since 2010, two more women have served as Supreme Court justices.

of meeting the quota.[4] Moreover, the Electoral Court would reject lists failing to comply with the quota. In the context of a closed-list proportional representation system, the placement mandate—guaranteeing that women would not be stuck at the bottom of lists—and the clear sanctions for non-compliance in a rule-bound culture served as a virtual guarantee that the quota would augment female representation. This would prove to be the case. The Uruguayan quota led women's representation in the Senate to double and women's share of seats in the Chamber of Representatives to increase to slightly over 18 percent.

Political elites recognized that the quota had succeeded in getting more women into office. When asked about the increase in women's numbers in parliament, a political party president simply explained: "well, if it weren't for the gender quota, that just wouldn't have happened" (Interview, August 5, 2015). As one female senator stated: "If you are asking me if I'm in the Senate because of the quota, then I have to tell you that yes, if there had been no quota, then I almost certainly would not be in the Senate. I would have been in a good spot on the deputy list" (Interview, August 10, 2015). A deputy did not mince words: "I'm here because of the quota" (Interview, June 2, 2015). A member of the Electoral Court pointed out specific women that would never have ended up in parliament were it not for the quota (Interview, July 7, 2016).

While political elites acknowledged the quota and its outcomes, our concern is with the visibility of the gender quota law among everyday Uruguayans. As we theorize in Chapter 2, the visibility of the quota could have important effects for citizens' political engagement and support. Establishing a relationship between the passage or implementation of gender quotas and citizens' political connectedness requires that we first assess whether citizens are in fact aware of gender quotas.

The (Lack of) Visibility of the Gender Quota

Uruguay trailed many of its neighbors in its adoption of gender quotas. Quotas had become commonplace in Latin America, and by 2009 not only

---

[4] As in many other countries of the world, officeholders in Uruguay are elected alongside a short list of alternates (known as *suplentes* in Spanish), who step in for officeholders in cases of illness, travel, or resignation of seats. Often these substitutes fill in only briefly for officeholders. However, if officeholders resign their positions then they permanently turn over their seats to *suplentes*. See Beckwith 1989 on how these positions could potentially be used to increase women's political participation, and refer to Hinojosa and Vijil-Gurdián 2012 for a discussion of how political alternate positions can also be used to subvert gender quotas.

had countries begun to increase their quota thresholds to 40 percent, but the first parity laws were being adopted in the region (Piscopo 2016).[5] Despite the region-wide use of gender quotas, we find that there was a general lack of awareness of the quota in Uruguay.

To ascertain whether citizens knew of quotas, we took a three-pronged approach. First, we asked respondents in our panel survey about their knowledge of the gender quota. Ours is the first academic study that addresses this relationship head-on by asking citizens about awareness of gender quotas. Second, we utilized interviews to assess the impressions of elites regarding citizen awareness of the gender quota. We carried out interviews in Montevideo with female members of parliament, political leaders, and civil society representatives during 2015 and 2016. Third, we also undertook content analyses to understand the visibility of the gender quota. We monitored newspaper coverage of the gender quota from 2001 through October 26, 2014 (election day) in three major publications. *El País, El Observador*, and *La República* were selected because these three papers have the largest circulations (*World Press Review; Press Reference*). These newspapers also mirror the ideological spectrum, with *La República* representing the left, *El País* occupying the center, and *El Observador* representing the right. We used Lexis-Nexis and the newspaper websites' internal search features to find articles using a range of search terms. The following sections examine each of these approaches in turn.

Our survey gauged awareness of the gender quota by asking respondents a two-part question. We asked individuals: "Are you aware of any measures to increase women's presence in parliament?" If respondents answered this question affirmatively, we asked: "What is this measure to increase women's representation called?" We avoided simply asking whether our respondents knew that a gender quota would be used in the upcoming elections. Such a question, we reasoned, would likely garner many false positives, as respondents sought to appear more knowledgeable in front of the interviewers.[6] The phrasing of our two-part question was specifically

---

[5] Not only was Uruguay late to adopt gender quotas, but the law itself limited their use due to the inclusion of an "expiration date." The law was to be applied only for the 2014 legislative elections. This was not wholly unusual; the first quota law in Mexico had also included a sunset clause. Chile also adopted a gender quota that includes an expiration, but Chile's quota law will not expire until after 2029 (Quota Project). In 2017, Uruguay re-adopted a gender quota without an expiration date.

[6] Questions regarding knowledge of quotas are infrequent, but when they have been asked usually are phrased like this question from the Brazilian Institute of Public Opinion and Statistics (IBOPE 2009; question 17): "Did you know or have you heard that there is a quota policy that requires that Brazilian political parties must have 30 percent of their seats for each elective position filled by female candidates?"

designed to avoid false positives and yet give respondents credit for knowing about the gender quota even if they could not specifically remember what such a measure was called. Emma Watson, a British actress best known for her role in the *Harry Potter* movies, had visited Uruguay to push for gender quotas, so some respondents answered the question with a reference to laws that Emma Watson had pushed for. We counted these as correct answers.

A few non-academic surveys have attempted to evaluate whether citizens know of gender quota laws in their own countries. These provided us with little optimism that Uruguayans—despite being a well-educated population—would know of the gender quota. Htun and Jones 2002 reported that three-quarters of Peruvians were unaware of the gender quota; the same percentage of Brazilians admitted that they did not know of their country's gender quota, which had been in force for more than a decade (Wylie 2018). Only 18 percent of Panamanians claimed knowledge of their gender quota (UNDP 2007).

Unsurprisingly then, we found limited knowledge of the gender quota. Prior to the 2014 elections, only 10 percent of our respondents knew of the quota. Following the application of the quota, a larger—but still limited—proportion of respondents knew of the gender quota: 15 percent.[7] Prior to the implementation of the quota, women were significantly less likely than men to be able to identify the law, but after implementation, the gender difference in quota knowledge disappears.

To better understand who was more aware of the quota law, we built a multivariate logistical regression model in which we examined several factors. The dependent variable is dichotomous: 1 indicates the respondent correctly identified the quota law. We expect that respondents who pay more attention to the news are more likely to be aware of the quota. Gender is measured with 1 indicating women and 0 indicating men, and thus we expect a negative relationship with men more aware given that men typically score better in political knowledge (Fraile and Gomez 2017a). We also control for political ideology, which is measured with a 10-point scale, with 1 signifying the most leftist and 10 the most rightist ideology. We expect that leftists may be more aware of the gender quota

---

[7] The careful reader may be concerned that we primed our survey respondents by asking about awareness of the gender quota in the first wave of the survey. However, as explained in Chapter 1, the panel survey included 469 fresh respondents. We asked the fresh respondents the same question about quota awareness as our panel respondents, giving us confidence that our results are not due to priming: an even greater number of the fresh respondents were aware of the gender quota than our panel respondents (21 percent).

than others due to a greater commitment to gender equality by the left. We also expect a positive relationship between awareness and age, education, and income. Further, those who are married and those who attend religious services more frequently may be more aware of the gender quota due to potentially stronger ties to community and discussion networks.

Table 4.1 reports the coefficients for each of these variables in predicting respondents' awareness of the quota measure before (Time 1) and after (Time 2) the implementation of the quota law. Importantly, women were significantly less likely than men to know of the quota law before the law is used for the first time. However, after implementation there is no statistically significant difference between men and women in their awareness of the quota, all else being equal. In addition, people who pay attention to the news were more likely to be aware of the quota law at both time periods. Importantly, those who hold a more leftist ideology are more likely to be aware of the quota at both points in time. We find that people with higher levels of education and those who are older are more likely to know about the quota law during both waves of the survey. In a different fashion, marital status was insignificant before the election but statistically significant after.

We supplemented the panel survey data with elite interviews. Our interviewees confirmed that there was limited public awareness of the

TABLE 4.1 Explaining Awareness of the Gender Quota

	TIME 1	TIME 2
Gender of Respondent	−.516 (.218)*	−.242 (.240)
Pay Attention to News	.066 (.014)***	.082 (.016)***
Political Ideology	−.089 (.042)*	−.117 (.048)*
Education	.057 (.007)***	.050 (.008)***
Income	−.002 (.005)	−.004 (.005)
Age	.309 (.115)*	.304 (.131)*
Married	−.171 (.094)	−.216 (.107)*
Religious Attendance	.016 (.012)	.021 (.015)
Constant	−2.163 (.096)***	−1.718 (.105)***
N	1173	710
Percent Correctly Predicted	89%	85%
Nagelkerke R Square	.243	.262

NOTE: The model uses logistic regression. The dependent variable is a binary variable with 0 indicating that the respondent did not know about the gender quota and 1 indicating that the respondent knew of the quota. Each cell contains the unstandardized coefficients, with standard errors (in parentheses) and level of statistical significance. ***p<.001; **p<.01; *p<.05.

gender quota. Functionaries of the state-run National Institute for Women noted that, "The topic didn't really resonate when they passed the law" (Interview, July 8, 2016). The individuals working for the National Institute for Women were finely attuned to the quota but did not feel that it received much general attention. One of them stated, "I didn't really hear much resistance in the media; there were some articles in favor, some against of course, but I didn't see much" (Interview, July 8, 2016). Some of these women believed that a lack of knowledge of the quota might have limited opposition to the quota: "I don't think there was much resistance to the quota in the general population, but I don't know if that's because people just didn't know about the quota" (Interview, July 8, 2016).

Similarly, we found little reason to believe that the quota amassed much visibility from our content analysis of major Uruguayan newspapers. Despite an exhaustive search for articles on gender quotas published in three main newspapers from 2001 until October 26, 2014, we obtained only 245 articles.[8] This indicates a general lack of coverage of gender quotas. Coverage of the quota, as expected, did rise during the time period when the quota was debated and passed (more than four of every 10 articles analyzed were from 2008 and 2009) and then again in the time period more immediately preceding implementation of the gender quota. On average, then, there were less than 19 articles about the quota per year published across the major newspapers.

Here, in examining news articles only and not opinion pieces (where we would expect to see variation in coverage of the quota based on ideology), we see important differences in the source of information, since those people reading the leftist *La República* were exposed to nearly four times as many articles (113) as those reading *El Observador* (28). Readers of *El País* were exposed to 67 articles. Again, this is the total number of news articles about the quota over the course of nearly 13 years. While the number of articles is small, our study does demonstrate important variability in quota coverage across the major newspapers. But importantly, our findings point to limited coverage of the gender quota prior to its use in the 2014 elections. The lack of quota awareness among the general population was not surprising given this limited media attention.

---

[8] For our analysis, we relied on the newspapers' own search engines and Lexis-Nexis.

A Visible Break with the Past: Seeing More Women in Office

It is important to separate visibility—or in this case, absence of visibility—of the gender quota from the visibility (or potential lack thereof) of women's descriptive representation in Uruguay. Even if citizens were unaware of the mechanism by which women's numbers in legislative office had increased, they might still notice that there were suddenly more women in politics. We sought to understand whether women's greater levels of descriptive representation obtained visibility. Did citizens know that there were now more women in political office?

Women's numbers in the Senate doubled following the 2014 elections, but this was not the only change to women's descriptive representation. President Tabaré Vázquez, who took office in 2015, increased women's presence in cabinet posts by appointing women to five of the 13 cabinet-level positions in the country. Women were appointed to the following posts: Ministry of Tourism, Ministry of Education and Culture, Ministry of Social Development, Ministry of the Environment, and Ministry of Energy.[9] Vázquez divulged his cabinet picks shortly after results of the November 30, 2014 runoff election were announced, meaning that our survey respondents might also have been seeing more women in politics due to the announcement of the new cabinet ministers, even though these women would not be taking their new posts—just like senators—until February 2015. This change to the cabinet would have added more female faces to Uruguayan politics and would have further enhanced the descriptive representation of women.

Our methodology for determining the visibility of descriptive representation consisted of three parts. First, we sought to assess visibility via our panel survey of Uruguayan citizens. Second, we relied on elite interviews carried out with female parliamentarians, other political elites, and leaders of civil society organizations. These interviews were conducted in 2015 and 2016. Third, we once again used a content analysis to monitor newspaper coverage of descriptive representation (using the same three newspapers

---

[9] Barnes and Taylor-Robinson expect that the symbolic effects that accrue from having women in these ministerial positions are "more likely when women are appointed to the most high-prestige or inner circle cabinet posts" (Barnes and Taylor 2018: 231). Barnes and Taylor-Robinson define these high-prestige and high-visibility posts as being defense, finance, and foreign relations. Women did not hold any of these positions in Vázquez's government. Similarly, work by Escobar-Lemmon and Taylor-Robinson 2016 indicates that women in Vázquez's cabinet were not given the choice ministries.

as for the quota analysis: *El País, El Observador*, and *La República*). This media analysis helped us understand what people were seeing in the weeks after the elections.

Understanding the Uruguayan Case

Before turning to the data from the panel survey, the elite interviews, and the content analysis, we first provide background to understand visibility in the Uruguayan case. As we explained in Chapter 3, understanding visibility requires an in-depth analysis of the political context.

As previously mentioned, the 2014 elections brought substantial changes in women's representation to the Senate (where women's representation increased from 13.3 percent to 26.7 percent) but minimal change to the Chamber of Representatives (which saw an increase from 15.2 percent to 18.2 percent).[10] These differences between the two chambers were the result of parties' efforts to minimally comply with the quota and the small size of districts for the lower house.[11] While the placement mandates had powerful effects in the larger districts, in the smaller districts the fact that the third position on a list often became the "women's spot" meant that women would effectively be sitting in unelectable places on a list.[12] Due to the large number of lists in departments with small district magnitude, it is rare for any list to have more than two safe seats. Because parties complied minimally with the law (Johnson 2015), women often appeared

---

[10] Women's descriptive representation increased further in the months after the election, as individuals vacated their seats to take cabinet-level positions in the new administration. A year after the parliamentary inauguration, women occupied 33.3 percent of the seats in the Senate and 20.2 percent in the Chamber of Representatives.

[11] By minimally comply, we mean that parties rarely did more than meet the exact requirements spelled out by the gender quota (for details on the Uruguayan parties' minimal compliance, see the thorough work presented in Johnson 2015). This is typical where quotas have been adopted (see, for example, Hinojosa and Piscopo 2013). Political elites had anticipated such minimal compliance. A former deputy who had been instrumental to the passage of the quota law noted: "we already knew that we'd get results in the . . . Senate; and if we move forward with parity, we'll get results there, but never in the Chamber of Representatives" (Interview, June 12, 2015).

[12] Our elite interviews made clear that parties and party leaders viewed the third place on a list as the "women's spot." A female senator explained that "in the logic of quota compliance, the third spot would go to a woman, never the second, and certainly not the first" (Interview, June 10, 2015). One political party elite felt that there was a "hurtful" attitude that women should go in the third spot (Interview, June 5, 2015). A senator from the *Frente Amplio* said: "they never think, we have to put a man among every three candidates. No, we have to put in a woman. And so the reasoning is that all the spots on the list that are multiples of three—3, 6, 9, 12—these spots are for the women" (Interview, June 10, 2015).

in unelectable third spots on the list. In the Senate, there is a single national district. There are fewer total lists and hence a larger number of individuals on each list are elected. Therefore, women were effectively represented in winnable spots on lists (i.e., whereas the #3 spot might be unelectable on a number of lists for the lower chamber, it would be an electable spot on a Senate list).

Not only were there differences in the percentages of women elected to the Chamber of Representatives and to the Senate, there were also long-standing differences between the two chambers. These differences, which we explain in detail below, make the upper chamber—where women's numbers doubled after the 2014 elections—the more visible chamber.

First, the Uruguayan Senate is made up of 30 members that are elected from a single nation-wide district. The Chamber of Representatives, on the other hand, has 99 members that are elected from 19 subnational units known as departments. Unlike deputies that represent departments in the Chamber of Representatives, senators have no geographic ties. The fact that the upper chamber is elected in a single district itself means that senators are national representatives. Since deputies are elected from the departments, they are unlikely to obtain national renown.

Second, there are considerable differences in the prestige attached to these two chambers. While the rise in women's representation in the lower house was minimal, the Senate is the more important chamber. The prominence of the position is reflected in the age requirements: to be a senator you must be 35 years old, whereas to be a deputy you need only be 25. As a member of the Electoral Court explained, "legally, they're legislators and just as important because their votes matter, but in the collective imagination, a senator is more than a deputy. That's just the truth. As a matter of fact, there's 30 of them and 99 deputies, which says a lot" (Interview, July 7, 2016). With only 30 senators versus 99 deputies, senators have greater "individual influence" than deputies and are much more well-known to the population. We would expect the more important position to be the more visible position as well. As a woman from one state agency explained, "There's something else that's the truth, and that's that deputies in this country have little visibility. The deputies with a lot of visibility, well, it's because they are leaders, party leaders . . . or they are running for another position. Deputies, in and of themselves, don't have much visibility" (Interview, July 8, 2016). Morgenstern notes that Uruguayan senators must be individuals with "national prestige" and González explains that the Senate is composed of the "highest stratum of the political elite" (Morgenstern 2001: 242; González 1993: 99 as cited in Bottinelli 2008: 30). Senatorial positions are undeniably the more coveted posts, and the "most visible dimension of a Uruguayan faction (or *sublema*) is a list for the national Senate, which is usually shown below the names of presidential candidates on the ballot" (Moraes 2008: 168).[13]

Finally, this discrepancy in visibility between the two legislative bodies may also be a function of the duties of each chamber. The Uruguayan Senate "resemble[s] the North American model" rather than those models "where the upper chamber has no (or limited) veto power over legislation" and where "upper chambers normally have less relevance than lower chambers" (Llanos and Sánchez 2006: 136). Llanos and Sánchez explain that Uruguayan senators are more powerful than their counterparts in the lower house; they note that senators have "greater individual influence" and find that senators are likely to be older than deputies, more likely to be male, and more likely to have a university education (Llanos and Sánchez 2006: 137–141).

The visibility of descriptive representation in the Uruguayan case does not simply vary by chamber, but is also a function of the electoral system. First, the use of closed-list proportional representation changes the visibility of these legislative positions. In closed-list systems, voters cast a ballot for a party list (or party faction list, in the case of Uruguay). The party ranks its candidates. In open-list systems, voters cast a ballot for a list but also for a candidate, giving voters the ability to influence who among those on their party's list is actually elected.

Closed-list proportional representation systems effectively minimize the connection between voters and candidates and therefore between citizens and legislators (Clucas and Valdini 2015). In closed-list systems, voters are less likely to develop personal connections with candidates. This lack of personalization means that during campaigns, voters would be less likely to even know the candidates competing for office, since they are not casting ballots for individuals but rather for parties. Campaigns are rarely focused on individuals in closed-list systems, and when they are, the focus is on those at the very top of the list.[14] Where voters have more intimate connections with their candidates and representatives, we would expect greater visibility.[15] For example, in countries like the United States,

---

[13] As will be discussed later in this chapter, the greater importance of the Senate position was unambiguous when one woman chose to renounce her seat in the Senate to take a seat in the Chamber of Representatives instead.

[14] Those individuals at the top of their party list come to be seen as the "face" of the party, sometimes quite literally, as in South Africa, where the person in the number one spot has their photograph appear next to the party name on the official ballot (Clucas and Valdini 2015).

[15] This also means that Uruguay is a hard test of our theory.

citizens have a single candidate that they will vote for in a congressional election; voters should be more likely to recognize the name of an individual that they have cast a ballot for.[16]

Second, Uruguay has a byzantine electoral list system that may also have implications for the visibility of legislators. Unlike in most closed-list proportional representation systems, in Uruguay each political party represents multiple "closed and blocked lists that compete among themselves within the party. Intra-party competition softens the rigidity of closed and blocked lists and transforms the Uruguayan system into a kind of intra-partisan preferential vote" (Altman and Chasquetti 2005: 240). The lists that voters see then are not actually party lists, but rather party faction lists.

The faction list system leads to a head-spinning number of lists. Although only seven parties competed in the 2014 elections, there were 548 lists presented for the Chamber of Representatives (Johnson 2015). The enormous number of lists further dilutes the visibility of candidacies for the Chamber. For the Senate, there were only 39 lists. Voters are simply more likely to know of individuals running on Senate lists, and therefore more likely to perceive a change to the gender makeup of these lists.

To complicate matters further, parties and factions may run the same individuals across multiple lists, and often do, placing their biggest names on numerous lists. The practice of fielding the same candidate for multiple positions can give women a tremendous visibility boost. The *Frente Amplio* placed Lucía Topolansky at the top of many of its lists,[17] something that was notable; the head of a feminist civil society organization explained that the *Frente Amplio* referred to these lists headed up by Topolanksy as "women's lists" (Interview, July 7, 2016). At the time, Topolansky was not only the First Lady of Uruguay but was also one of the most distinguished

---

[16] In Uruguay it would be inappropriate to carry out the kind of work that in the United States has attempted to assess whether descriptive representation matters for various measures of symbolic representation. The scholarship on the United States has regularly looked at how having a female candidate for an important—hence visible—political position impacts citizens. This type of candidate-centric analysis makes little sense in the context of closed-list proportional representation, the use of a single, national district for the election of senators, and the repetition of some names across multiple lists when it is clear that one individual will not represent multiple districts.

[17] For the *Frente Amplio*'s National Convention, the largest faction in the *Frente Amplio* (known as *Espacio 609*) placed Lucía Topolansky at the top of all of its lists. As Johnson 2016 points out, this would make it appear as if more than 45 percent of the faction's winning candidates were female; however, given that Topolansky would be unable to serve in more than one position, it was actually—in all but one case—her political alternates who would be entering the National Convention (Johnson 2016: 409).

politicians in the country, having received the most votes of any senatorial candidate in 2009.[18] Topolansky was not the only woman who appeared multiple times across lists. The repetition of the same (female) names assured these individual women greater visibility but also made it appear as if women were more present than ever in Uruguayan politics. While individuals, like the aforementioned Lucía Topolansky, who headed many lists would garner substantial visibility, the sheer number of lists and candidates in this closed-list proportional representation system likely limits the visibility of other candidacies.

Assessing Visibility via a Panel Survey

Our survey not only assessed knowledge of the gender quota but also inquired about women's descriptive representation to gauge visibility.[19] We asked the following questions:

- *What percentage of the Senate is female?*
- *Do you know what the percentage of female senators will be in the new Senate that takes office in February?*
- *Do you believe that women's representation in parliament is too low, just right, or too high?*
- *Is there a senator or deputy that you feel represents you well or that you admire?*[20]

Previous work has attempted to assess whether citizens know how well represented women are in legislative bodies. For the United States, Sanbonmatsu 2003 examined awareness of women's representation

---

[18] Topolansky, like her husband, had become active in politics in her youth, joined the Tupamaro guerrilla group, and been imprisoned during the dictatorship. Later she co-founded her political party. She had served five years in the Chamber of Representatives and then been elected in 2005 to the Senate. She was re-elected in 2009 and 2014.

[19] Here, it is important to note that we cannot separate out the effects of increased descriptive representation of women as candidates versus as elected officials who have not yet taken office. We could not separate out these effects given that it would be impossible to carry out another wave of our survey after most campaigning had concluded but before election results were announced. This type of survey, after all, takes weeks to carry out, and the campaign period in Uruguay is limited. As previously noted, the complete list of candidates was only announced about six weeks before the elections.

[20] Because campaigning had begun when we asked this question in Wave 1, we expect that the campaign season itself primed individual's responses. In other words, we expect that due to the larger number of female candidates participating in the election, we would receive more female names than we would have received had we asked the question a year in advance of the election.

and found very limited knowledge of the actual percentages of women in Congress. Only two percent of her sample was able to properly state that 12 percent of congressmembers were women.[21] We also ask our respondents about the percentage of women in legislative office.

It is worth noting that due to the factors mentioned above—as well as to the fact that women's representation in Uruguay's parliament is considerably higher than it was in the United States Congress at the time—this is actually a harder question for Uruguayans than it would have been for Americans responding to Sanbonmatsu's survey. With hundreds of lists, it can take days to initially figure out who has been elected.

Moreover, measuring visibility by asking citizens the percentage of women in office is further complicated in the Uruguayan case due to substitutions. Legislative elections come a few short months before departmental (subnational) elections. Members of parliament will often run for these departmental positions, first ceding their seats to their alternates in order to campaign and then (if they win their elections) resigning their seats permanently to take a new position. Since legislators are regularly plucked from their legislative seats to take on cabinet-level and other non-elected posts in the new administrations (both presidential and departmental), this means that there can be significant turnover in parliament between the October elections and July of the following year. As previously mentioned, the use of political alternates also complicates matters, as legislators may cede their seats to alternates. To be clear, the number of women in parliament changes over time, and especially in the first year after the legislative elections. This can make it difficult for everyday citizens to know the percentage of women in political office.

Nonetheless, we find that our respondents do perceive that women's representation is higher after the 2014 elections. In the first wave of our survey, we asked our respondents to tell us what percentage of the Senate was female. After the election, we then asked our respondents to tell us what percentage of the newly elected Senate was female—and to provide

---

[21] Using this five percentage point range (10–15 percent) as a correct answer meant that Sanbonmatsu coded 29 percent of the sample as providing a correct answer to this question, rather than 2 percent. In Sanbonmatsu's study, women were more likely than men to overestimate women's congressional representation. Sanbonmatsu 2003 demonstrated that individuals who overestimated the percentage of women in the US Congress were less likely to support increasing women's representation. Ignorance about women's representation can "erode support for increasing women's representation because respondents are more likely to overestimate women's representation than to underestimate it" (Sanbonmatsu 2003: 379). In other words, the lack of awareness of women's actual levels of descriptive representation has consequences for policy preferences.

their best guess if they were uncertain.[22] We find that in the first wave, the average response was 14.60. For the panel respondents, in the second wave, the average was 17.55. For the fresh respondent. in Wave 2, on the other hand, the average was 19.42. These differences indicate that people did see an increase in women's representation. The individual responses to these questions vary broadly, but these averages across time do tell an important story. Panel respondents were less likely to be correct about true levels of women's representation in the Senate than the fresh respondents, indicating that we did not prime our panel respondents.

While individual responses were grossly inaccurate, between the first and second waves of the survey we can see that the percentage of people believing that women's representation was quite low (between 1–10 percent) drops substantially. In the first wave, 54.5 percent of respondents pegged women's representation in the Senate as being between 1–10 percent, while in the second wave that percentage drops to 38.8 percent. The percentage of respondents estimating women's representation between 11–20 percent stays about the same, but the percentage of individuals who believe that women make up between 21–30 percent of the Senate goes up from 12.9 percent to 20.7 percent. While our respondents were unaware of the exact percentages of women in the Senate, they knew that women's representation had increased. The most commonly provided answer in the first wave was 10. In the second wave, the most frequently given answer was 20.

Further evidence of the visibility of changes to descriptive representation is captured in Table 4.2. We asked our respondents to tell us whether, in their opinion, women's representation in parliament was too low, just right, or too high. Women's views of representation in parliament became significantly more favorable (i.e., they became more likely to say that women's representation was just right and less likely to say that it was too low) after implementation of the gender quota.[23] In comparison, men's views of women's representation did not change between the two time periods. Because women's views changed between the two time periods while men's remained stable, the gender gap in these assessments of women's representation disappears. Here we can see that prior to the

---

[22] The interviewers were instructed to press for a guess if individuals seemed reticent to answer the question. As Espírito-Santo and Verge have noted, previous studies "have not proven that citizens are aware of the gender composition of political institutions" (Espírito-Santo and Verge 2017: 495).
[23] According to the paired t-test, the difference in women's views of representation of women in parliament between Time 1 and Time 2 is statistically significant at p<.01.

TABLE 4.2 Assessment of Women's Representation in Parliament

	TIME I		TIME 2	
	MEN	WOMEN	MEN	WOMEN
Women's representation in parliament is . . .				
Too Low	63%	72%	63%	62%
Just Right	35%	26%	35%	36%
Too High	2%	2%	2%	2%

election, a greater percentage of people thought that women's representation was too low. This change in the percentage of individuals saying that women's representation is no longer too low is the result of perceived changes to descriptive representation that took place between the two waves of our survey. After the election, women still believe that women's political representation is too low, but the differences between the first and second waves indicate that female citizens noticed a change to the descriptive representation of women. Interestingly, it is women's assessments that change. Men's assessments of women's representation stay constant, but women perceive that women's representation in parliament is now more equitable.

Additionally, we asked respondents in both waves of our survey to name a legislator they admired. In the first wave, among the 335 respondents who provided a response, female senators were mentioned 84 times, including Senators Lucía Topolansky, Constanza Moreira, and Mónica Xavier. A total of seven unique women senators were named. Thus, in the pre-election survey 25 percent of the admired senators were women. After the election, 31 percent of the senators mentioned were women (116 of a total of 374). Senator Lucía Topolansky topped the list as the most frequently mentioned senator, with a wider variety of female senators receiving mention as well—from Constanza Moreira to María Elena Laurnaga to Macarena Gelman to Zulimar Ferreira. A total of 12 unique women senators were named. This too provides evidence of increased visibility of female politicians.

Unlike the gender quota, which received little attention prior to its use in the 2014 elections, there was considerably more awareness of women's increased descriptive representation. As we explained in our theoretical chapter, if the gender quota were visible we could assume that any effects to citizen engagement could be the result of the quota itself and not due to its effects, namely the increased descriptive representation of women. We could imagine that the quota could introduce positive effects, as it could signal to citizens—and in particular, to female citizens—that their government cares about their representation and inclusion.

Since we found, however, that the gender quota was largely invisible, then any effects to political engagement that we find are *not* the result of the gender quota itself. This would certainly be in keeping with the findings of Kittilson and Schwindt-Bayer 2012, who examined the effect of passage of the gender quota in Uruguay (their analysis came prior to the application of the quota), and found no changes to political engagement.

Elite Perceptions of the Visibility of Descriptive Representation

We also relied on interview data to understand public awareness of changes to descriptive representation following the 2014 elections. While our interviewees had expressed reservations that the general public knew about the gender quota, they nonetheless believed that use of the quota had important effects: "I think the success of the quota was that it put the topic into public debate. If it weren't for the quota law the topic of women's participation in politics wouldn't have been part of the debate; it was the kicker in creating a sensitivity [to women's political participation]. That sensitivity wasn't there when the quota law was being debated" (Interview, June 8, 2015).

In fact, some felt that the increased dialogue about women's underrepresentation ultimately made people more aware of the quota itself: "I think that since the election more people know about the quota . . . previously no one knew about it" (Interview, July 8, 2016). Much of this dialogue was a result of the Bianchi scandal and created a larger conversation about women's political representation.

The Bianchi scandal emerged because the quota law did not prevent factions from running the same woman for seats on multiple lists and in both chambers simultaneously. This allowed women to cede seats to male alternates (see Johnson 2015) and thereby limited the success of the quota. Since the Uruguayan quota did not stipulate that *suplentes* must be of the same sex as the individuals for whom they would substitute—which is now the law in Mexico—these substitutions led to changes in the percentage of women in parliament and importantly were used as a tool to undermine the gender quota (Hinojosa 2017). Parties could run women candidates to meet the quota and then have them resign their seats to their male alternates. In 2014, these substitutions garnered much attention in Uruguay; specifically, one woman—Graciela Bianchi—was placed in electable positions on both lists as part of an effort to subvert the gender quota.[24]

The case of Graciela Bianchi attracted significant scrutiny. While it was not unusual for individuals to run for seats in the Chamber of Representatives at the same time that they competed for seats in the Senate, this case was unusual in that Bianchi occupied the third-place spot on both lists. This meant that she was running in safe seats on both lists.[25] Traditionally, individuals running on both lists would be placed in more precarious spots, possibly combining a safe seat in the lower house with placement on the upper house list that was likely unelectable. The fact that Bianchi occupied the third spot was telling, as this was the "woman's spot"; that is, in order to (minimally) meet the quota, the party would need a woman to occupy the third spot on the list. She fulfilled this function on both the list for the Chamber of Representatives and on the list for the Senate, which meant that if elected to both positions—and again, these were both considered safe seats—she would need to cede one of her positions, something that was "publicly condemned by feminist organizations as a tactic to by-pass the quota law" (Johnson 2016: 409).

Bianchi not only won both seats and had to permanently renounce one of her seats, but she opted to relinquish the more important and more coveted seat in the Senate rather than leave the seat in the Chamber of Representatives to an alternate. This too caused alarm. Bianchi was criticized for running in both positions and abandoning the more important post (Johnson 2016), but there was no doubt that this was an agreement with the *Partido Nacional* and not simply her own decision.

When asked about the Bianchi case, one woman working for the National Institute for Women simply noted that "it was quite symbolic" (Interview, July 8, 2016). A deputy was less restrained in her assessment: "That's just wrong. It's not right. It's not good. You shouldn't do those things . . . well, there were colleagues that were willing to do that sort of thing, but they are clearly not

---

[24] In 2015, however, these substitutions ultimately proved beneficial for women. Women's numbers in parliament increased due to these replacements. For a historical analysis of how women have fared due to the use of these substitutions, see Johnson 2015 and Johnson 2018.

[25] For the 2014 elections, there were three women that were simultaneously elected to the Senate and the Chamber of Representatives. In the weeks following the elections, political parties decided which seats individuals would take; ultimately, 18 female deputies took office as did eight female senators. The case of Bianchi attracted the most attention because she opted to take the less prestigious position.

committed to this cause . . . those spots that they took in the Senate list and the deputy list, those could have gone to a woman. But renouncing those seats means that a woman's not going to have that seat" (Interview, June 2, 2015).

Female members of parliament and other political elites that were interviewed routinely brought up the Bianchi case without prompting despite the fact that interviews were carried out 6–18 months after Bianchi announced her decision. Bianchi was a "public embarrassment" (Interview, June 12, 2015). From these interviews, it was evident that the Bianchi scandal had brought widespread attention to women's descriptive representation in Uruguay. As a former leftist legislator stated, Bianchi had been "completely chastised by the media" (Interview, July 3, 2016).

Gauging Coverage in the Media

Just weeks before the 2014 elections, the United Nations Development Program sponsored a training program for female candidates. Program analyst Virginia Varela stated "the situation is ripe for women to stop being 'invisible' to the electorate . . . and the media needs to be able to 'see' them" (PNUD 2014). Were the media able to see women?

We sought to measure the visibility of increased descriptive representation through our content analysis. The coding of descriptive representation for this project covered the time period after the elections and continued until the newly elected parliament took office on February 15, 2015.[26] We used the same three newspapers for this portion of the analysis and used search terms to find relevant articles that discussed any increases in women's presence in elected office. Thirty-one search terms were used.[27] A total of 41 news articles were coded.[28] We found that

---

[26] The content analysis of quota coverage did not overlap with this coverage. The content analysis specific to the coverage of the gender quota concluded on election day, while this coverage began on election day.

[27] The search terms used were: *cuota femenina, cuota política, cuotificación, cuota legislativa, ley de cuotas, ley de cuotificación, cuota de género, ley 18.476, ley de representación femenina, norma femenina, norma de cuotificación, representación femenina, representación de mujeres, cuota mujeres, cuota partidaria, integración de mujeres, integración política, integración femenina, debate cuota femenina, debate cuota política, debate ley de cuotas, implementación cuota política, implementación cuota femenina, implementación ley de cuotas legisladoras, participación de las mujeres, participación femenina, bancada femenina, participación política de las mujeres, porcentaje de mujeres, perspectiva de género,* and *representación equilibrada.*

[28] While these numbers may seem low, they are in keeping with findings by Campbell and Wolbrecht 2006 on the United States. They did an event count from *The New York Times* of articles that "specifically draw attention to a female politician's gender" and found that in an average year there were 11.6 such articles published, with a range of 0 to 34.

women's descriptive representation garnered about seven times more news coverage than the gender quota (approximately 10 articles per month for descriptive representation versus about 1.5 articles per month for the quota). Eight of these appeared in *El Observador*, 12 appeared in *El País*, and 21 appeared in *La República*. In other words, the most extensive coverage of women's descriptive representation came from the paper of the left, and the least extensive coverage came from the paper of the right. In addition to the 41 news articles that were coded, we also coded 12 opinion pieces that appeared in these papers during the time period being examined. Half of these appeared in *La República*. Approximately half of all articles (both news articles and opinion pieces) on descriptive representation mentioned the role that the gender quota itself played in guaranteeing the new, higher levels of women's descriptive representation.

The content analysis that we undertook provides us with only a partial view into how the media covered the boost to women's descriptive representation. Given that recent work indicates that political learning is most successful when information is disseminated via TV infotainment programs (Ferrín, Fraile, and García-Albacete 2019), we supplement this analysis of newspaper coverage by also including information from television news shows, as well as social media coverage, that drew attention to women's presence.

The Bianchi scandal was not the only way in which the media displayed greater female political presence. Numerous photographs of the group of women that would be part of the new parliament circulated that would have also made visible women's representation. One article from *Subrayado* (10/28/2014) was specifically on women elected to the Senate and to the Chamber of Representatives. The article was posted to Facebook and received more than 420 comments and even more likes. A news program segment on "Quota laws spark debate about women in politics" was posted the month after the election and garnered more than 200 views. A number of news circulated with the general tagline of "Get to Know the New Faces in Parliament"; readers or viewers were sure to notice that many of those new faces were the faces of women (*Teledoce* 11/20/2014).

As previously mentioned, the case of Graciela Bianchi attracted much media attention. While the attention was negative—focused on how this undermined the spirit of the quota law and was an affront to women— it did have the positive effect of calling attention to increases in women's descriptive representation generally.

Even prior to the elections, the media had noticed that Bianchi was likely to win both seats and therefore likely to renounce one of those seats to a male alternate. An article appearing in *La República* quoted public intellectual and political science professor Niki Johnson of Uruguay who stated: "I want someone to find a man who would be willing to give up his seat in the Senate to take a seat with much less status and power in the Chamber of Representatives" (Thove 2014). Moreover, women's organizations not only argued that the *Partido Nacional* was attempting to evade the quota by placing Bianchi in two electable positions but that "a previous deal had been made prior to the election so that Bianchi would take the less prestigious position" (Pérez 2015: 22). When it was clear that she had won both spots, Bianchi was subjected to even more media scrutiny (*Teledoce* 1/28/2015).

Graciela Bianchi's announcement on January 27, 2015 confirming that she would be resigning her Senate seat in favor of her male alternate and instead assuming her seat in the Chamber of Representatives led to a flurry of activity. In *El Observador*, this was referred to as "publicly mocking the quota law" (Garcé 2015). Senator Martha Montoner immediately called for a new quota that would prevent this from happening in the future and started working on a legislative proposal (*El País* 1/28/2015). Even fellow party members publicly expressed their disappointment with this decision. Verónica Alonso, for example, said, "I don't see it as something positive. It's like a bit of cheating" (*El País* 1/28/2015). In interview after interview, Bianchi argued with her critics, stating that she was a "free woman" and that "no one tells me what to do" (*Televisión Nacional Uruguay* 2/16/ 2015).

Bianchi further drew attention to herself. For example, on the day of her announcement, she tweeted, "Why is it so hard for so many women to understand that some women make their own decisions?" Bianchi has more than 14,000 followers on Twitter (the current Uruguayan president has half this many followers, as does the previous, very popular president José Mujica), meaning that this message received significant attention.[29] This was a pointed comment, meant to indicate that she was not being forced by her party to resign the more important position but instead was making this decision voluntarily. She attracted more attention to her peculiar situation because of comments such as these.

---

[29] It is important to note that Uruguay is a small country of less than 3.5 million people.

The media was not solely focused on Bianchi. One news broadcast from *Televisión Nacional Uruguay* featured an interview with *Partido Nacional* leader Luis Lacalle Pou; while the interview was ostensibly about extending the franchise to citizens living abroad, Lacalle Pou received a barrage of questions about placing Bianchi in electable spots for both chambers. Lacalle Pou reiterated that he "complied with the law" (*Televisión Nacional Uruguay* 11/21/2014).

Two years later, Graciela Bianchi was still being mentioned in reports; her case in particular spurred proponents of the gender quota, who were hoping to pass new quota legislation, to consider the ways the law applied in 2014 had allowed "cheating" to take place (Gil 2017). As new legislation was being considered, the news media were rehashing the Bianchi scandal: "The most notorious case was that of Graciela Bianchi, who gave up her seat in the Senate in order to take a spot as a deputy for the *Partido Nacional*" (Delisa 2016). From the attention that Bianchi received through the traditional media and also through social media, it was clear that this controversy highlighted the gender makeup of the parliament.

Conclusion

Women's absence from politics may send the "implicit message that politics is about men—and, therefore, for men" (Verba, Burns, and Schlozman 1997: 1064). Women's presence in politics can change this message but only if it is visible, as explained in Chapter 2. The visibility (or lack thereof) of gender quotas and descriptive representation in Uruguay is an important element of our story. Uruguayan citizens, we have established in this chapter, were not aware of the gender quota. It was insufficiently visible and therefore could not affect political engagement and support. However, the descriptive representation of women in politics following the 2014 elections was a visible change. While Uruguayans did not know exactly how many women would occupy Senate seats in the upcoming legislative session, they were aware that women were better represented in parliament than they had previously been. Women were less likely to say that women's parliamentary representation was "too low" than they had been just a few short months earlier. As one senator explained, "It's an undeniable reality in a body with only 30 members . . . that there's more women. In a panning shot of a session of the Senate, you are seeing more women; in a commission, you are seeing more women . . ." (Interview, June 10, 2015). In the chapters that follow, we assess how this "undeniable reality" affected citizens' political engagement and support.

CHAPTER 5 | Piquing Political Interest, Forging
Political Engagement

ENGAGED CITIZENS ARE essential to the democratic process not only because they participate and voice their demands to elected officials, but
also because they shape the salience of political issues on the agenda and
structure the debate surrounding these issues. Gender differences in political engagement raise concerns about deficits in democratic discourse and
agenda setting.

This chapter focuses on the effects of increasing numbers of women
in elected office on women's and men's engagement with the democratic
process. As the prior chapter demonstrated, the visible strides made by
women in the 2014 Uruguayan election make this country the ideal laboratory in which to assess the consequences of women's presence in office
for political engagement. Here we examine how women's presence shapes
gender differences in political interest, knowledge, discussion, and citizens' perceptions of their own efficaciousness. These measures underpin
the propensity to engage with politics in a meaningful way.

These attitudes and activities tap different dimensions of political engagement and are related to one another in important ways. Figure 5.1
depicts the relationships among the dimensions of political engagement
that we examine. First, individuals who are initially interested in politics
are more likely to seek out and acquire political knowledge. The strong
relationship between political interest and knowledge holds across Latin
America (Fraile and Gomez 2017a). And those with greater political
knowledge are more likely to feel like they can understand important political issues. Political interest also heightens the likelihood that a person
will enter into a political discussion. A sense of political efficacy also
encourages individuals to participate in political discussions.

Seeing Women, Strengthening Democracy. Magda Hinojosa and Miki Caul Kittilson, Oxford University Press (2020).
© Oxford University Press. DOI: 10.1093/oso/9780197526941.001.0001.

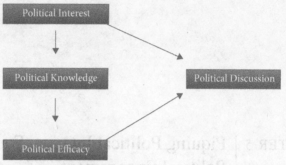

FIGURE 5.1 Dimensions of Political Engagement

To track gender differences in these measures of political connectedness over time, we draw on our unique survey in Uruguay before the gender quota is used for the 2014 elections—and, therefore, before the resulting increase in women's descriptive representation—and after the increase in women's descriptive representation. We also take a closer look at the effects of age and gender.

As detailed in Chapter 2, we theorize that the quota law and subsequent visible jump in women in elected office is the primary factor influencing changes in political engagement. Women's growing numbers in the legislature may symbolize a more open and inclusive political system. While jumps in women's presence in office may positively affect men's and women's engagement with the political process, we expect women in the electorate will be more powerfully influenced by these changes than men.

Gender gaps in political engagement across Latin America are often attributed to differential resources and socialization among men and women (Fraile and Gomez 2017a). First, as individuals develop the cognitive skills and resources to navigate the political arena, they are more likely to engage politically in fundamental ways. Women historically had less formal education than men; but today in Latin America, gender disparities in education levels have largely been eliminated across the region. Only in Guatemala are boys more likely than girls to be enrolled in secondary schools. By the mid-1990s, women made up 48 percent of university students in Latin America and, at present, women outnumber men in university classrooms (Hinojosa 2012; UNESCO 2019). Education is one of the strongest indicators of political interest, knowledge, efficacy, and political discussion (Verba, Schlozman, and Brady 1995; Solt 2008). Second, income also relates to political engagement, as low levels of income may limit the time and energy to devote to following political news.

In some ways, income may act a proxy for occupation, which is linked to obtaining skills that can translate into political engagement (Verba, Schlozman, and Brady 1995). Third, research shows that those with stronger, wider networks are more likely to engage in politics (Klesner 2007). Community ties are often cultivated through religious service attendance or marriage. Fourth, it is also commonly expected that being older is related to greater political engagement as individuals gain more information and ties to the political world over subsequent elections (Fraile and Gomez 2017b).

These gendered differences in resources and socialization have been theorized to affect the types of gender gaps that we are interested in explaining. Consequently, it is vital to ascertain whether gender differences remain after controlling for these resource- and network-based factors. Importantly, paying attention to political news is a known influence on piquing political interest, acquiring political knowledge and confidence in navigating the political realm, and then discussing politics.

Gender Differences in Political Engagement Pre- and Post-Election

First, we examine whether the jump in women's presence in elected office heightened interest in politics. In our survey, we ask respondents at each wave of the survey, "How much interest do you have in politics: a lot, some, little, or none?" We recoded these response categories so that higher numbers indicate more political interest, and present the average response for men and for women before and after the election.

As the data in Figure 5.2 demonstrate, during the first wave of the panel, men are significantly more interested in politics than women, as expected. However, the gender gap in political interest closes after the jump in women's representation in elected office. Women's interest in politics appears to be enhanced by the uptick in women's presence in positions of power.

Does this same pattern hold when we control for other influences on political interest? In a multivariate analysis, we control for how much respondents pay attention to political news, as well as their education, income, age, marital status, and religious service attendance. We expect and find that each of these factors enhance the degree of political interest. In addition, we control for left/right political ideology and expect a negative

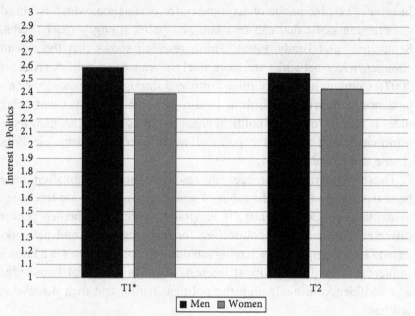

FIGURE 5.2 Changes in Political Interest
NOTE: ***p<.001; **p<.01; *p<.05.

coefficient, as those who report a more leftist ideology may be more polit-ically interested given that the government at this time was leftist. Due to the ordinal nature of the response categories, we employ a logistic ordinal regression.

A multivariate analysis to predict political interest supports our bivariate findings: men are significantly more politically interested than women be-fore the election. However, when these same respondents are interviewed after women's numbers in office jump, gender is no longer a statistically significant influence, as demonstrated in Table 5.1. In both the first and second waves of the survey (T1 and T2), statistically significant variables include political ideology and education. Age is only statistically signif-icant at the first time point—with older individuals being more likely to be politically interested—and paying attention to the news is statistically significant only after the election. In contrast to our expectations, we find no statistically significant relationships for the remainder of our control variables.

Second, we examine gender differences in political knowledge before and after the election. The political knowledge scale is created by adding up the number of correct responses to three factual questions. The questions used in the scale follow the LAPOP surveys. First, respondents were

TABLE 5.1 Explaining Political Interest

	TIME 1	TIME 2
Gender of Respondent	−.319 (.111)**	−.265 (.147)
Pay Attention to News	.094 (.008)	.083 (.010)***
Political Ideology	−.097 (.020)***	−.172 (.027)***
Education	.628 (.132)***	.813 (.166)***
Income	.002 (.002)	−.001 (.003)
Age	.220 (.057)***	.140 (.078)
Married	−.014 (.045)	.020 (.062)
Church Attendance	−.001 (.008)	.016 (.012)
Threshold 1	−.454 (.199)**	−1.411 (.275)**
Threshold 2	1.421 (.201)***	.999 (.266)***
Threshold 3	2.844 (.214)***	3.082 (.292)***
Model Chi-Square	272.65	168.010
−2 Log Likelihood	2910.66***	1609.935***
DF	8	8
Pseudo R-Square (Cox and Snell)	.207	.212
N	1176	706

NOTE: The model uses logistic ordinal regression. Each cell contains the unstandardized coefficients, with standard errors (in parentheses) and level of statistical significance. ***p<.001; **p<.01; *p<.05

asked, "What is the name of the current president of the United States?" Next, they were asked, "How many departments does this country have?" Finally, respondents were asked, "How long is the presidential term of office in this country?" The political knowledge scale ranges from 0 to 3, where 0 indicates no correct responses and 3 indicates the respondent correctly answered all three questions.

For political knowledgè, rather than presenting the results from our panel respondents at Time 2, we use the results based on the fresh sample of respondents. Using the panel respondents at both time points would introduce the possibility that respondents interviewed during the first wave of our survey had sought out the answers to the questions prior to being queried again in the second wave. Therefore, we compare the political knowledge of respondents pre-election with an entirely new set of respondents after the election.[1]

[1] In Figure 5.3, Time 3 denotes the 469 fresh respondents included in the second wave of the survey. These respondents were queried during the same period of time as the panel respondents. We use Time 3 in order to compare the averages of two groups who are being asked these questions for the first time: one before the election and the other group after. Appendix 1.1 provides more information on this group.

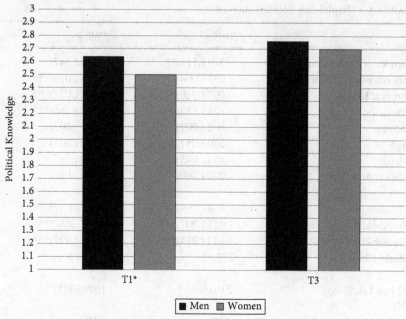

FIGURE 5.3 Changes in Political Knowledge
NOTE: ***p<.001; **p<.01; *p<.05.

Figure 5.3 presents the average scores for men and for women on the political knowledge scale. Before the election, men were significantly more knowledgeable about politics than women. This gender gap in favor of men's higher political knowledge in Uruguay supports previous research (Fraile and Gomez 2017a). The educative effects of the election campaign and heightened salience of politics render both men and women more knowledgeable after the election. Following the election, men are still slightly more knowledgeable about politics, but the difference is substantively smaller and no longer statistically significant.

We next move to test these results in a multivariate model where we can control for a host of other potential influences.[2] The results of the multivariate ordinal regression are presented in Table 5.2, and confirm the

---

[2] To assess these effects for differences among men and women, we tested several interaction terms but found few statistically significant results. Both men's and women's reactions may vary with partisanship, but a large number of respondents did not give their party affiliation, limiting our ability to test this question with these data. In addition, sample size limits our ability to properly test some important overlapping sources of privilege and disadvantage. Looking at questions of intersectionality is especially complicated in Uruguay given the very small numbers of Afro-Uruguayan or indigenous citizens: less than 5 percent of the population is black and about half that many are indigenous.

TABLE 5.2 Explaining Political Knowledge

	TIME I	TIME 2
Gender	−.453 (.133)***	−.244 (.259)
Political Interest	.267 (.071)***	−.019 (.157)
Pay Attention to News	.094 (.020)**	.024 (.016)
Political Ideology	.025 (.024)	−.047 (.043)
Education	.025 (.005)***	.010 (.009)
Income	.003 (.003)	.016 (.035)
Age	.199 (.067)**	.441 (.147)**
Married	.068 (.055)	−.135 (.102)
Religious Attendance	−.011 (.008)	−.025 (.112)
Threshold 1	−1.209 (.333)***	−3.506 (1.056)***
Threshold 2	.274 (.290)	−1.933 (.923)**
Threshold 3	2.031 (.290)**	.190 (.894)
Model Chi-Square	135.909***	1669.015***
−2 Log Likelihood	2037.232	521.928**
DF	9	9
Pseudo R-Square (Cox and Snell)	.112	.047
N	1170	411

NOTE: The model uses logistic ordinal regression. Each cell contains the unstandardized coefficients, with standard errors (in parentheses) and level of statistical significance. ***p<.001; **p<.01; *p<.05.

bivariate findings. Even after controlling for a host of socioeconomic and associational factors, before the election men are more politically knowledgeable than women, and this difference is statistically significant. This finding bolsters the multivariate results of Fraile and Gomez who control for a similar set of "motivation, resources and ability" variables (2017a: 100). After the election, accounting for the same conventional explanations, gender is no longer a statistically significant indicator of political knowledge.

As depicted in Figure 5.1, we expect that those who are politically interested in the first place are more likely to acquire and value political information. Consequently, we have added political interest to the model. Political interest is a statistically significant influence on political knowledge before the election, but loses this significance after the election. Through the experience of the election, political information is salient and disseminated. Given the rise in political knowledge across the board, this knowledge is no longer as concentrated among the politically interested after the election.

Among the control variables, political interest, education, and paying attention to the news are statistically significant before the election but not after. After the campaign ends, political knowledge is both higher and more evenly distributed. The propensity to be interested in politics and having the education to seek out sources of information and make sense of them are no longer statistically significant influences. At both time points, age is a statistically significant indicator, with older people having more political knowledge than younger individuals.

Third, we examine feelings of understanding of political issues as a measure of internal political efficacy. Like political interest, feelings of understanding of political issues constitute an important prerequisite for political discussion and for participation (Verba, Burns, and Schlozman 1997). We asked respondents on a scale from 1 (strongly disagree) to 7 (strongly agree) how much they agreed or disagreed with the statement: "You feel you understand the important political issues of this country."

Similar to the pattern with political interest, Figure 5.4 shows that men express significantly more confidence in their understanding of issues during the first wave of the survey than their female counterparts.

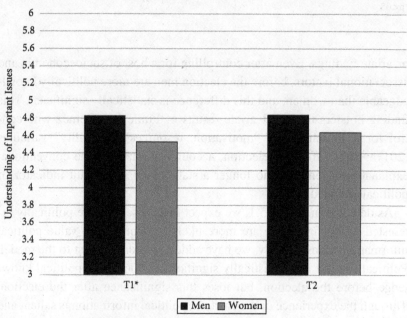

FIGURE 5.4 Changes in Understanding of Important Issues
NOTE: ***p<.001; **p<.01; *p<.05.

TABLE 5.3 Explaining People's Understanding of Important Issues

	TIME 1	TIME 2
Gender of Respondent	−.317 (.093)***	−.205 (.118)
Political Knowledge	.187 (.067)*	.173 (.093)
Pay Attention to News	.048 (.005)***	.027 (.007)***
Political Ideology	−.060 (.017)***	−.045 (.021)*
Education	.022 (.003)***	.018 (.004)**
Income	−.004 (.002)*	.000 (.002)
Age	.301 (.047)***	.006 (.063)
Married	.026 (.038)	.100 (.050)**
Religious Attendance	.001 (.007)	.013 (.010)
Constant	2.541 (.228)***	3.294 (.304)***
R-Square	.212	.116
N	1172	706

NOTE: The model uses OLS regression. Each cell contains the unstandardized coefficients, with standard errors (in parentheses) and level of statistical significance. ***p<.001; **p<.01; *p<.05.

However, by the second wave—after the implementation of gender quotas and the jump in women's numbers in elected office—we no longer see a significant gender gap in how men and women perceive their understanding of the important issues facing Uruguay. Importantly, on average, men's reported understanding of issues remains the same from the pre- to post-election surveys. The change in internal efficacy is evident only among women, whose average reported understanding rises from 4.53 to 4.64. Although this is a relatively small change on a 7-point scale, it is enough to render the gender gap as no longer statistically significant.

The multivariate analyses presented in Table 5.3 similarly reveal statistically significant differences in men's and women's levels of confidence in their understanding of important issues before the implementation of the gender quota law. However, and consistent with the bivariate results, after the election we find no gender differences in men's and women's self-assessments of their understanding of the important issues facing the country.[3]

The models control for the respondent's levels of political knowledge. We find that the political knowledge scale is statistically significant in the pre-election model (Time 1), but not in the post-election model (Time 2).

---

[3] Consistent with the panel data, we find no gender difference among the new cross-section of respondents in assessments of their understanding of issues.

Thus, factual knowledge is an important predictor of perception of understanding political issues before the election, but after the election these two are unrelated. Paying attention to political news is a statistically significant variable at both points in time. Naturally, tuning into political news makes a person much more likely to feel that they can understand the important political issues of the day. In addition, those with a leftist political ideology profess more internal efficacy. This is likely due to the fact that a leftist government was in power at the time of the survey, and supporters of leftist parties thus feel more able to understand the political issues facing the country.

Among the socioeconomic control variables, education is statistically significant at both points in time. We expected marriage would encourage political engagement generally, and by extension, political efficacy. Those individuals who are married report more internal efficacy in the post-election survey than those who are not married. Conversely, income and age are only statistically significant at Time 1. The shifting significance of these control variables most likely means that they tap similar life stage indicators. As citizens mature into later stages in life, they may be more likely to marry and have higher incomes. Simultaneously, they will experience more election campaigns and become exposed to more political information.

Next, we explore how the increase in women's presence in elected office affects political discussion. In our survey, we ask respondents at each wave of the survey: "How many days last week did you talk about political news with friends, family, or learn about it through informal channels?" After the national elections, fewer people may be having political discussions, although some may still be discussing the election outcomes. Importantly, we are not interested in the levels of political discussion, but we instead focus on the differences between men and women at each point in time.

As the data in Figure 5.5 demonstrate, there is little difference between men and women at either point in time. Men and women are equally likely to engage in political discussion. Before the election, both male and female respondents are more likely to be talking about politics than after the election. The mobilization and news media attention to politics during the campaign spurs more discussion than occurs after the election is over. Importantly, when it comes to political discussion, gender differences are minimal and show uniform change pre- and post-election.

But does gender matter after we control for our standard battery of influences? Table 5.4 presents the results of an OLS regression modeling the number of days within the last week that respondents report discussing

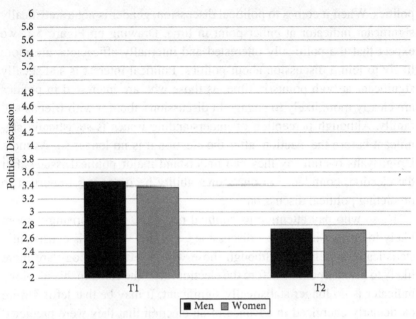

FIGURE 5.5 Changes in Political Discussion
NOTE: ***p<.001; **p<.01; *p<.05.

TABLE 5.4 Explaining Political Discussion

	TIME 1	TIME 2
Gender of Respondent	−.195 (.138)	−.123 (.183)
Political Interest	.681 (.078)***	.537 (.106)***
Political Efficacy	.128 (.046)**	.079 (.062)
Pay Attention to News	.096 (.008)***	.055 (.011)***
Political Ideology	−.069 (.025)**	−.054 (.033)
Education	.007 (.005)	.013 (.006)*
Income	.006 (.003)*	.005 (.004)
Age	.076 (.072)	.330 (.100)**
Married	−.024 (.056)	−.067 (.077)
Religious Attendance	.002 (.010)	−.002 (.015)
Constant	−.570 (.309)	−.879 (.419)**
R-Squared	.309	.183
N	1163	693

NOTE: The model uses OLS regression. Each cell contains the unstandardized coefficients, with standard errors (in parentheses) and level of statistical significance. ***p<.001; **p<.01; *p<.05.

politics. When it comes to political discussion, gender is not a statistically significant indicator at either point in time. Drawing on Figure 5.1, we expect that the politically interested and internally efficacious are more likely to join a discussion about politics. Political interest is statistically significant at both points in time, as those who are interested in politics are clearly more likely to engage in discussions about it with friends and family. Although perception of understanding issues is statistically significant before the election, after the election it is no longer so. As more Uruguayans overall say they can understand major political issues after the election, confidence in one's own ability becomes less important to predicting political discussion.

Those who pay attention to political news are, not surprisingly, more likely to engage in political discussions, and this variable is consistently statistically significant. Although those with a leftist ideology are more likely to discuss politics before the election, after the election this ideology indicator is no longer statistically significant. It may be that leftists were particularly energized in advance of an election that they were predicted to win.

Among the socioeconomic control variables, those with more education are more likely to discuss politics after the election, and the relationship with income is statistically significant only in the pre-election survey. Older people are more likely to discuss politics at Time 2, while being married and attending religious services exert little influence.

Does Age Matter? Analyzing Political Engagement

As explained in Chapter 2, previous studies suggest that younger people may be more receptive to the symbolic effects of big gains in women's presence in elected office. During the formative political years, new circumstances may have a larger impact, since younger individuals "are in the process of learning about the political world and their place within it, and thus their actions may be particularly open to influences in their environment" (Wolbrecht and Campbell 2007: 924). By contrast, for older citizens new events are layered upon years of exposure to the political arena, thus previous experience makes them resistant to any effects (Wolbrecht and Campbell 2017). Moreover, older individuals have established their ways of engaging with politics and may be less malleable. However, Fraile and Gomez find a different pattern across generations in their analysis of political interest. Cues about gender equality "contribute to bridging the gender gap in political engagement only during adulthood" (2017b: 601). Thus, we test whether the effects from before the election to after the election are stronger among those under the age of 30.

Given the centrality of political interest and political efficacy to all dimensions of political engagement, as depicted in Figure 5.1, we focus on those two dependent variables to examine these relationships for those 30 years old or younger. For both young men and young women, levels of political interest are lower overall than they are in the population as a whole. Yet the results mirror those of the entire population. Before the election, men report being more interested in politics than women, and this gap is statistically significant. However, after the election, the gap is no longer statistically significant. Post-election, both men and women are more politically interested, and women's political interest grows more steeply than men's. Importantly, the effects are not more pronounced among those 30 and under than for the total population. The online appendix (available at: http://www.public.asu.edu/~mhinojo1/books.html) includes a figure reporting the average level of political interest for young men and women before and after the election.

We also examined changes in understanding of important issues among those who are 30 and under (a corresponding figure is available in the online appendix). Overall reported levels of understanding issues are slightly lower among young people than the broader population. But just as with the broader population, among those 30 and under, more men than women report understanding of important issues before the election. The statistically significant difference disappears after the election, and men and women report similar levels of internal efficacy. Among young women, the average level of reported understanding of important political issues goes from 4.13 before the election to 4.6 after the election. Both groups grow in their perceived ability to understand issues, but women's levels increase sharply. As with political interest, this change is not more pronounced among young people, but rather looks similar to the population overall.

Conclusion

Simply put, the overall pattern is one of rising engagement for women as a consequence of the changing face of representation. After the election, previously statistically significant gender gaps in favor of men evaporate for political interest, political knowledge, and perceptions of understanding issues. For political discussion, the lack of gender differences carries over to after the election. Across a variety of measures of political engagement, the shift is unmistakable: women become more engaged with the democratic process after the visible jump in women in elected office.

Further, these contours are replicated for young people for the most fundamental aspects of political engagement: political interest and understanding of issues. Although the gender differences are not exaggerated among younger people as we had expected, the effects are similar for young people and the population at large.

Our multivariate models build upon themselves as we add political interest and perceptions of understanding major issues to subsequent dimensions of political engagement. And even still, our findings of decaying gender differences in political engagement hold. Importantly, this change from before to after the election is not a function of gender differences in resources such as income or education, nor stage of the life cycle. Instead, the electorate appears to react to the election outcome and, as a consequence, women relate to politics in a different way than they had before. Across a wide array of measures, women's engagement grows.

While this chapter focused on engagement with the process, there are other orientations that may be affected by women's increased presence in office. In the chapter that follows, we examine how the visible rise of women in political office affects how female citizens connect with politics in a different way, by examining gender gaps in trust and support for the political system.

CHAPTER 6 | Inspiring Trust in Institutions, Building Political Support

SUPPORT FOR DEMOCRACY is essential to building its legitimacy (Easton 1975). Higher levels of political support form the basis for democratic legitimacy and speak to the health, vibrancy, and durability of democracy. In contrast, low levels of support may pose a threat to the stability of the political system (Lipset 1959).

Given the traditional exclusion of women from the political realm, we can expect that women as an outsider group hold different perspectives on government relative to their male counterparts. Contemporary gender gaps in political support may reveal continuing differences in the way men and women relate to the political process. By looking at respondents directly before and after a groundbreaking election, we aim to uncover some of the mechanisms that inspire trust and support, and how these mechanisms work differently for different people.

Only a handful of studies have investigated gender differences in political support, in part because the gaps are rarely large in magnitude. In the wake of democratic transitions in Central and Eastern Europe, researchers found some gender differences. Women displayed more trust in democratic institutions in Poland and Ukraine (Johnson 2005), but lower levels of support for the democratic regime across a wider variety of countries (Gibson, Duch, and Tedin 1992; Oakes 2002; Waldron-Moore 1999). Even without large gender gaps, being attentive to the ways in which elite-level change affects men's and women's political support is key to more fully understanding how representation affects political support among different groups of people.

An important body of established research has uncovered several influences on levels of political support. Those who support the winners of

Seeing Women, Strengthening Democracy. Magda Hinojosa and Miki Caul Kittilson, Oxford University Press (2020).
© Oxford University Press. DOI: 10.1093/oso/9780197526941.001.0001.

an election are (not surprisingly) more satisfied with the way democracy works (Anderson et al. 2005; Bowler and Donovan 2002; Singh 2014). Yet, the rules governing elections can condition this relationship. Blais, Morin-Chassé, and Singh 2017 demonstrate that "representation deficits" affect political support. While they find decreased satisfaction with democracy when seat shares and vote shares are misaligned, we believe a similar logic flows from descriptive representation. When voters do not see elected officials who share their characteristics, the democratic process and its institutions may not appear to live up to their ideals. Along these lines, Oakes suggests that the chasm between the values and ideals of democracy and the realities of women's severe underrepresentation in higher political offices "may cause women to feel alienated from the new democratic political system and to form more negative attitudes towards democratic principles" (2002: 163).

We build on earlier findings derived from cross-national snapshots connecting women's descriptive representation with higher levels of support for the legislature and democratic legitimacy (Norris and Franklin 1997; Karp and Banducci 2008; Schwindt-Bayer and Mishler 2005). But we take a different tack: we compare men's and women's reported levels of political support over time within one country. Further, we expect that with the jump in women's numbers in office, the rise in support for democratic institutions and democratic performance should be most evident among women in the electorate.

Conceptually, political support is composed of several dimensions that can be arrayed along a continuum from more specific support for current officeholders to more diffuse orientations toward democratic principles and basic attachments to the nation-state (Easton 1965). We focus on the "mid-range" of Easton's 1965 continuum from most specific to most diffuse support (Norris 2017). We do not examine support for current officeholders, because our survey purposely takes place before the newly elected parliament took office. This unique timing allowed us confidence in saying that any changes that we see in public support are not a result of changes in the policy arena, nor deliberate acts of representation. In addition, questions that assess trust in particular actors are less valid measures of political support than questions asking about institutions (Catterberg and Moreno 2005). Further, we do not have theoretical reason to expect the rise in women's legislative inclusion to affect an individual's sense of national identity. Indeed, women's gains represent democratic inclusion—potentially moving existing institutions closer to democratic principles.

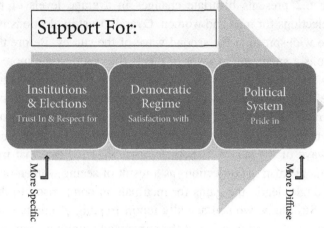

Support For:

Institutions & Elections	Democratic Regime	Political System
Trust In & Respect for	Satisfaction with	Pride in

More Specific

More Diffuse

FIGURE 6.1 Dimensions of Political Support

Figure 6.1 depicts the levels of political support examined in this chapter. First, we examine trust in several political institutions and elections by looking at citizen responses to a series of questions about their feelings toward government and elections. Second, we look at support for democratic performance. Finally, we examine pride in the political system, which is a slightly different way of assessing support for the regime (Dalton 2008).

Because the jump in women's presence operates as a symbol of democratic inclusion, changes in political support should be concentrated in measures of trust in elections, democratic values, and principles. In particular, we expect that changes in women's representation strengthen support for the institutions of the democratic regime or support for the political system itself. We expect that noticeable increases in women among elected officials is more likely to affect fundamental aspects of the political system. To test these ideas, we employ our panel survey of Uruguayan citizens to assess several measures of political support. We begin by focusing on the most specific level of support, moving from left to right across the dimensions of support illustrated in Figure 6.1.

Gender Differences in Political Support Pre- and Post-Election

We start our analysis by examining trust in elections, which is crucial to citizen participation and electoral integrity. Respondents were asked in both waves of the survey, "Using a scale where 1 means 'not at all' and 7 means 'a lot,' to what extent do you trust elections?"

Figure 6.2 presents bivariate changes in average levels of reported trust in elections for men and women. Overall, trust in elections is higher and more widespread at the second wave of the survey. Before the election there is a small gap in favor of men, who demonstrate more trust in elections. However, the gender difference is not statistically significant. After the jump in the number of women in elected office, both men and women trust elections more than they did before the 2014 elections. The fact that both men and women exhibit increased trust in elections in the second wave of the survey is notable, as it may indicate that men also become more trusting in elections as a result of seeing women obtain office (although clearly the gains for men pale in comparison to those for women). Strikingly, women actually report trusting elections more than men in the post-election wave of the survey, although this gender difference is not statistically significant.

We expect that a variety of factors shape an individual's trust in elections and that gender is only one among them. We therefore control for the standard battery of variables consistent with the previous chapter. Citizens who are tuned into elections and politics more generally also demonstrate greater support for the political system, a relationship that

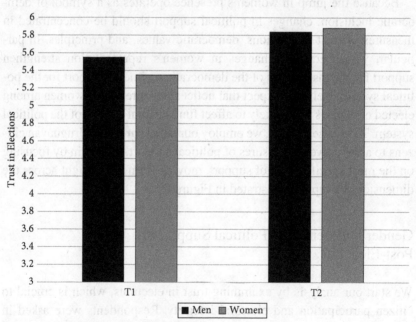

FIGURE 6.2 Changes in Trust in Elections
NOTE: ***p<.001; **p<.01; *p<.05.

works reciprocally (Anderson et al. 2005). Thus, those who pay more attention to political news may be more likely to exhibit trust in elections.

Importantly, respondents who support the winning candidates and parties are more likely to say that they trust the election process (Anderson and LoTiempo 2002) and are satisfied with democracy (Anderson et al. 2005; Bowler and Donovan 2002). In the case of Uruguay, the incumbent party, the *Frente Amplio*, retained the presidency and maintained its majorities in the Senate and Chamber of Representatives. Given that the *Frente Amplio* is the only major leftist party in the election,[1] we use respondents' political ideology to capture their alignment with the winners of the election. We expect those with a leftist ideology to profess greater political support.

Although demographic variables show inconsistent effects in predicting trust and support in past research (Anderson et al. 2005; Citrin and Stoker 2018; Anderson and Guillory 1997), we follow previous research by including them in our multivariate models. Specific to this research, resources such as education and income are more likely to be accrued by men than women, and so we control for these factors as well. In general, younger people tend to be less trusting of political authorities and institutions (Dalton 2008). Therefore, we control for age and expect older respondents to be more supportive. We do not control for other demographic variables—such as race or ethnicity—due to the very small number of Uruguayans who identify as indigenous or as Afro-Uruguayan.[2]

In their review of research on political trust, Jack Citrin and Laura Stoker write that the "most promising explanation for change in trust is politics itself" (2018: 57). Consistent with this, we are interested in the reaction of Uruguayans to a change in the political context: the sea change in women's election to office.

So how does the relationship between gender and trust in elections change before and after the jump in women's representation, all else being equal? The unstandardized coefficients from this OLS regression model are presented in Table 6.1 in Appendix 6.1. Supporting our expectations

---

[1] The other major parties, including *Partido Nacional* and *Partido Colorado* are all center or center-right parties. Our survey did query individuals regarding their party affiliation. We use a measure of ideology rather than party affiliation due to the (1) large number of people refusing to provide their party identification; and (2) vast majority of respondents aligned with the major leftist party and only small numbers of people aligned with other political parties.

[2] We are constrained in our ability to look at intersectional questions in our analysis because of the low numbers of indigenous and Afro-Uruguayans. Over multiple waves of the LAPOP survey between 2010–2016, between 1.4–2.8 percent of the population identified as indigenous, and between 2.7–3.3 percent identified as black.

and the bivariate findings, the importance of gender in shaping trust in elections wanes from the pre- to post-election surveys. Before the election, men are significantly more trusting of elections. After the jump in the number of women elected, gender is no longer a statistically significant indicator of trust in elections.

In addition, we expect that those who pay more attention to political news will trust elections more strongly. This expected relationship holds before the election but not after. Given the success of the leftist parties in the election, those individuals with a leftist ideology should place more trust in elections. At both points in time, this relationship is statistically significant.

Among the socioeconomic characteristics, education is related to trust in elections at the first time point, and older people are more trusting at both points in time. In summary, as trust in elections rises across the board after the election, individual-level characteristics including gender and education are less important in shaping this orientation. The election experience appears to have eroded some of the inequalities in trust based on varying levels of education and political attentiveness.

We also queried our respondents about their trust in the Electoral Court. Created in 1924, the Electoral Court is an autonomous body which, according to its own website, serves as a "fourth branch" of government.[3] The Electoral Court is tasked not just with maintaining the national voter registry and therefore determining who is and is not allowed to vote, but also is the institution charged with determining who is and is not eligible to run for office. Political parties register their lists of candidates with the Electoral Court, and for the 2014 elections the Electoral Court was responsible for determining whether political parties' candidate lists were in compliance with the gender quota.[4] Additionally, the Electoral Court must interpret the law as it relates to electoral matters; for example, as a minister of the Electoral Court explained, the Electoral Court was compelled to determine how the gender quota would apply to alternate positions (Interview, July 7, 2016).

Since the Electoral Court regulates elections and electoral activities, we felt it was important to understand whether citizens trusted this institution. As voting is obligatory in Uruguay, and citizens over the age of 18

---

[3] https://www.corteelectoral.gub.uy/institucional/creacion_y_evolucion.
[4] Although the Electoral Court was charged with forcing party compliance with the gender quota, it has not itself historically been an inclusive institution. Between the return of democracy in 1985 and 2010, none of the Electoral Court's members were women.

are legally required to register to vote, all Uruguayans have direct interaction with the Electoral Court. A lack of trust in the Electoral Court would signal that citizens did not have faith in the electoral process.

While trust in the Electoral Court rises for both men and women from pre- to post-election, the increase for women is larger, as Figure 6.3 shows. Notably, before the election there is no statistically significant relationship between gender and trust in the Electoral Court. However, after the election women are more trusting of the Electoral Court than men, and the difference is statistically significant. Again though, there is some indication that men feel more confidence in electoral institutions following a sizable increase in women's parliamentary representation.

We also compare the role of gender on trust in the Electoral Court in a multivariate analysis, where we control for the same variables included in the previous multivariate analysis. Because our focus is on gender and we are less concerned about the control variables, the results of the multivariate model are presented in Table 6.2 in Appendix 6.1. When we control for other factors, gender is not a statistically significant indicator at either time point. Paying attention to political news, holding a leftist ideology, having more education, and being older are all statistically significant influences on trust in the Electoral Court—both before and after the election.

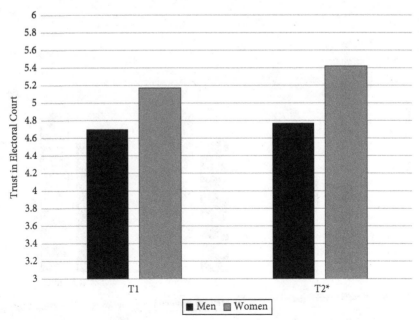

FIGURE 6.3 Changes in Trust in the Electoral Court
NOTE: ***p<.001; **p<.01; *p<.05.

With the election, the composition of the parliament changes appreciably, and this change is our focus. Therefore, we expect trust in parliament to increase, particularly among women in the electorate. Survey respondents were asked, "Using a scale where 1 means 'not at all' and 7 means 'a lot,' to what extent do you trust parliament?" Figure 6.4 presents reported levels of trust in parliament from this question.

Given that women's descriptive representation doubled in the Senate, and women made less substantial gains in the Chamber of Representatives, we asked about trust in the Senate and Chamber of Representatives separately in the second wave of our survey. We asked: "To what extent do you trust the Senate?" and "To what extent do you trust the Chamber of Representatives?" For these questions, once again, 1 is the lowest and means "not at all" and 7 is the highest and means "a lot."

After the election, trust in the Senate and in the Chamber is higher for men and women than the average trust in parliament before the election. And what about differences between men and women? Before the election, the difference in trust in parliament is not statistically significant. Importantly, after the election women report slightly higher levels of trust in the Senate than men, and this difference is statistically

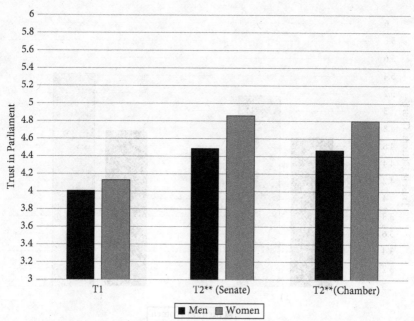

FIGURE 6.4 Changes in Trust in Parliament
NOTE: ***p<.001; **p<.01; *p<.05.

significant. Similarly, after the election the relationship between gender and trust in the Chamber of Representatives is statistically significant with women reporting slightly higher levels. Despite the larger gains in the Senate, women's trust increases in both the Senate and Chamber of Representatives. Once more, men too feel greater trust in parliament following the election. A corresponding table (Table 6.3) presenting a multivariate analysis is available in Appendix 6.1.

Do these changes in trust in electoral institutions and the legislative branch extend more broadly across the institutions of government? Respondents were asked about their trust in several political institutions. The scale runs from 1–7 for each of these institutions, as it had for the Electoral Court. We created a composite scale of trust in institutions, which is composed of scores for trust in the president, Supreme Court, municipal government, judicial system, and Electoral Court. This additive scale therefore ranges from 5 to 35. We checked the reliability of this index and found it to be acceptable, with Cronbach's Alpha of .77 for the first wave and .81 for the second.

We compare the bivariate relationship between gender and the index of trust in institutions of government, and the results are presented in Figure 6.5. Before the jump in the number of women, men and women

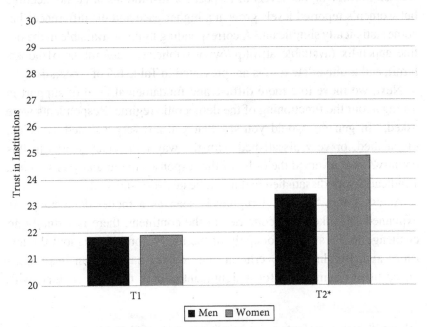

FIGURE 6.5 Changes in Trust in Political Institutions
NOTE: ***p<.001; **p<.01; *p<.05.

were similarly trusting in political institutions. However, after the election, while we see increases for both men and women, women report greater trust in political institutions. This relationship is statistically significant.

The multivariate analyses echo these findings, and Table 6.4 with these results is included in the Appendix 6.1. After controlling for a host of influences, gender is not a statistically significant factor at the first time point but becomes significant at the second point in time. In the wake of a large increase in women in office, women in the electorate trust political institutions more strongly than they did before the election.

Our survey also measured support for institutions with a different question, "To what extent do you respect the political institutions of Uruguay?" The same scale was employed, where 1 means "not at all" and 7 indicates "a lot." This question is purposefully broad, and respondents may be thinking of a variety of different institutions in their response. In this way, the concept of institutions is defined by the respondents themselves.

Respect for institutions follows the same pattern as our index of trust in political institutions. At the bivariate level, gender differences are statistically insignificant before the election and rise to statistical significance after the election. In the second wave of our survey, women report higher levels of respect for institutions than their male counterparts. Both men and women average higher levels of respect for institutions after the election, but women's reported levels grow at a higher pace and the differences become statistically significant.[5] A corresponding figure is available in the online appendix (available at: http://www.public.asu.edu/~mhinojo1/books.html), and multivariate results are presented in Table 6.5 of Appendix 6.1.

Next, we move to a more diffuse and fundamental level of support in asking about the functioning of the democratic regime. Respondents were asked, "In general, would you say that you are very satisfied, satisfied, dissatisfied, or very dissatisfied with the way democracy works in this country?" We reversed the order of the responses in our analysis so that a 1 indicates very dissatisfied and a 4 indicates very satisfied.

Across Latin America, Uruguay is seen as a model democracy. As explained, "Unlike other countries in the continent, there is virtually no challenge to the state's monopoly of the use of force throughout the territory and, by almost any criteria, the country has been an institutionalized liberal democracy for a significant part of the 20th century, with

---

[5] Multivariate analyses predicting respect for institutions at T1 and T2 are presented in Appendix 6.1. The coefficient for gender mirrors the bivariate relationship: no statistical significance at T1, but significant at T2.

political conflict and change following institutionalized and democratic procedures. Democratic institutions have been traditionally operated and political decisions have been processed by the proper popularly-elected authorities without constraints whatsoever on free and fair elections" (Altman 2008: 486). Uruguayans themselves recognize that their democratic system works well. Among all Latin Americans, Uruguayans express the most positive conceptualizations of democracy, equating democracy with freedom, equality, and participation in politics, and also have the highest levels of system support in the region (Millet, Holmes, and Pérez 2010).

Looking at the simple relationship between gender and reported democratic satisfaction in Figure 6.6, we report the average response for men and for women. We can see that the gender gap is not statistically significant at either point in time. Men and women not only report similar levels of satisfaction with democracy at both time points, but we see almost no change for men and women after the election. Table 6.6 in Appendix 6.1 provides results from the multivariate analysis.

At an even more diffuse and fundamental level is support for the political community, which can be measured by tapping feelings of pride in the political system. Our survey respondents were asked, "Using a scale

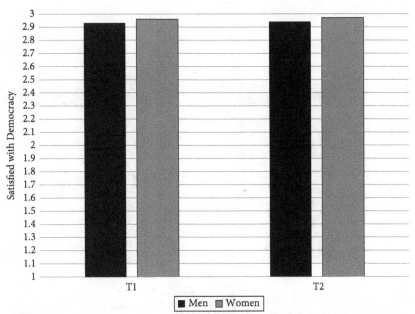

FIGURE 6.6 Changes in Satisfaction with Democracy
NOTE: ***p<.001; **p<.01; *p<.05.

where 1 means 'not at all' and 7 means 'a lot,' to what extent do you feel proud of living under the political system of Uruguay?"

When we look at the bivariate relationship between pride in the political system and gender, we find that pre-election there is little difference among men and women in their reported levels. After the election, women report greater pride than their male counterparts, and this difference is statistically significant. Here too we see rising levels of pride in the Uruguayan political system among men and women following the election of an unprecedented number of women to legislative office. Women's average level of pride grows more over this short period of time than men's, as shown in Figure 6.7.

It is important to control for additional potentially important influences on pride in the political system, and we present those results in Table 6.7 in Appendix 6.1. Even with these controls, the change in the role of gender in structuring pride in the political system supports our expectations. Before the election, men and women are not significantly different in their reported levels of pride in the political system. In contrast, after the election women are significantly prouder of their political system than men. Following the contours of previous analyses, paying attention to political news and a leftist ideology are both statistically significant influences at

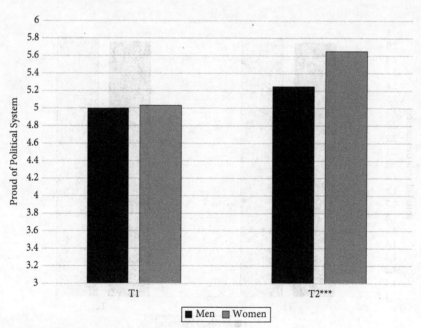

FIGURE 6.7 Changes in Pride in Political System
NOTE: ***p<.001; **p<.01; *p<.05.

both points in time. In addition, older respondents report greater pride in the Uruguayan political system.

Does Age Matter? Analyzing Changes in Political Support

Just as in Chapter 5, where we examined political engagement, our theory predicts that the effects of women's noticeable gains in the Senate may exert a stronger effect among young people. Because younger Uruguayans carry less baggage into the election, their orientations may be more malleable than those of older people.

We investigate whether the patterns we have uncovered for the electorate at large look different for young people. Among the variety of mid-level political support items we investigated for the total population in this chapter, we selected two items. One reflects a concrete measure (the elections themselves), and the other is a broader measure of political support (pride in the political system). For both young men and young women, trust in elections is slightly lower overall than for the total population. Gender differences are statistically insignificant both before the election and after. This pattern mirrors the relationship found for the population overall. Thus, young men are no more likely to trust elections in Uruguay than young women, and this effect is stable across the span of the election. A figure showing these changes in trust in elections among young people appears in the online appendix.

In a similar fashion, the bivariate patterns for those 30 years old and younger largely follow the pattern found for all Uruguayans. We also examine the change from before to after the election in pride in the political system. Pride in the political system remains stagnant for young men, but grows considerably for young women from the pre- to post-election waves of the survey. After the election, the gender difference in pride in the political system is statistically significant, with women reporting a greater sense of pride than men. The online appendix includes a figure examining changes in pride in the political system among young people.

Despite common expectations that young people may be differently affected by changes in the characteristics of their elected officials, the patterns among younger men and women largely follow the contours of the broader public. Therefore, our findings indicate that the effects of a sizable jump in women are more noticeably felt by women in the electorate regardless of their age.

Conclusion

Taken together, the findings of this chapter differ from the pattern uncovered in Chapter 5. Here we find that, overall, before the election there were few differences between men and women in their levels of political support. After the election, however, women's political support rose higher than men's levels, and in most instances this gap became statistically significant. Yet, just as in the previous chapter on political engagement, we find that the election of sizable numbers of women to political office fortifies women's political connections. And this pattern is consistent across a variety of measures, indicating that it is a robust finding and not an artifact of the way we measure political support.

In an era where many lament declining levels of political support, it is important to note that the driving forces behind political support may be gendered, albeit in subtle ways. In particular, women's political support is altered by a noticeable jump in women's election to office in Uruguay. On balance, men's levels of political support do not appear to change in the same ways as women's after the election.

The consequences of the changing face of elected officials in Uruguay offer some broader implications for democracy and representation. In the next chapter we turn to those broad themes.

APPENDIX 6.1

TABLE 6.1 Explaining Trust in Elections

	TIME 1	TIME 2
Gender of Respondent	−.276 (.098)**	.003 (.111)
Pay Attention to News	.026 (.007)**	.012 (.007)
Political Ideology	−.097 (.018)**	−.106 (.020)**
Education	.422 (.116)***	.220 (.124)
Income	.004 (.002)	.000 (.002)
Age	.338 (.051)***	.256 (.059)**
Married	.048 (.040)	−.038 (.047)
Religious Attendance	.008 (.007)	−.001 (.009)
Constant	4.543 (.173)***	5.530 (.196)***
R-Square	.124	.079
N	1176	707

NOTE: The model uses OLS regression. Each cell contains the unstandardized coefficients, with standard errors (in parentheses) and level of statistical significance. ***p<.001; **p<.01; *p<.05.

TABLE 6.2 Explaining Trust in Electoral Court

	TIME 1	TIME 2
Gender of Respondent	.055 (.106)	.173 (.117)
Pay Attention to News	.029 (.006)***	.014 (.006)*
Political Ideology	−.054 (.019)**	−.094 (.021)***
Education	.018 (.004)***	.012 (.004)**
Income	.003 (.002)	−.001 (.002)
Age	.417 (.055)**	.500 (.063)***
Married	.072 (.044)	−.050 (.050)
Religious Attendance	.001 (,008)	−.025 (.010)**
Constant	2.807 (.211)***	4.017 (.236)***
R-Square	.135	.153
N	1167	702

NOTE: The model uses OLS regression. Each cell contains the unstandardized coefficients, with standard errors (in parentheses) and level of statistical significance. ***p<.001; **p<.01; *p<.05.

TABLE 6.3 Explaining Trust in Parliament

	TIME 1	TIME 2
Gender of Respondent	.103 (.103)	.335 (.121)***
Pay Attention to News	.029 (.006)***	.017 (.007)*
Political Ideology	−.156 (.019)***	−.133 (.022)***
Education	.011 (.004)**	.005 (.004)
Income	.002 (.002)	−.003 (.002)
Age	.208 (.053)***	.259 (.065)***
Married	−.014 (.042)	−.031 (.052)
Religious Attendance	.001 (.007)	−.009 (.101)
Constant	3.43 (.204)***	4.190 (.244)***
R-Square	.112	.100
N	1170	699

NOTE: The model uses OLS regression. Each cell contains the unstandardized coefficients, with standard errors (in parentheses) and level of statistical significance. ***p<.001; **p<.01; *p<.05.

TABLE 6.4 Explaining Trust in Institutions

	TIME 1	TIME 2
Gender of Respondent	−.143 (.387)	1.364 (.471)**
Pay Attention to News	.119 (.026)***	.067 (.031)*
Political Ideology	−.746 (.069)***	−.713 (.085)***
Education	.844 (.465)	.017 (.525)
Income	−.005 (.007)	−.018 (.009)
Age	.841 (.200)***	1.223 (.254)***
Married	.131 (.159)	−.237 (.200)
Religious Attendance	.029 (.028)	−.068 (.039)
Constant	21.115 (.683)***	23.725 (.834)***
R-Square	.140	.145
N	1164	686

NOTE: The model uses OLS regression. Each cell contains the unstandardized coefficients, with standard errors (in parentheses) and level of statistical significance. ***p<.001; **p<.01; *p<.05.

TABLE 6.5 Explaining Respect for Institutions

	TIME 1	TIME 2
Gender of Respondent	.011 (.097)	.287 (.109)*
Pay Attention to News	.022 (.005)***	.017 (.006)**
Political Ideology	−.047 (.017)**	−.053 (.020)**
Education	.007 (.003)*	.000 (.004)
Income	−.005 (.002)*	−.001 (.002)
Age	.153 (.050)**	.195 (.058)**
Married	.056 (.040)	−.056 (.046)
Religious Attendance	.007 (.007)	−.011 (.009)
Constant	4.437 (.193)***	5.036 (.220)***
R-Square	.053	.048
N	1170	707

NOTE: The model uses OLS regression. Each cell contains the unstandardized coefficients, with standard errors (in parentheses) and level of statistical significance. ***p<.001; **p<.01; *p<.05.

TABLE 6.6 Explaining Democratic Satisfaction

	TIME 1	TIME 2
Gender of Respondent	.006 (.123)	.019 (.168)
Pay Attention to News	.016 (.007)*	.015 (.009)
Political Ideology	−.213 (.023)***	−.189 (.031)***
Education	−.001 (.004)	.007 (.006)
Income	−.002 (.002)	.004 (.003)
Age	.006 (.063)	−.094 (.089)
Married	.002 (.051)	.078 (.070)
Religious Attendance	−.001 (.009)	.013 (.013)
Threshold 1	−4.267 (.304)***	−4.138 (.426)***
Threshold 2	−2.293 (.264)***	−2.067 (.360)***
Threshold 3	1.009 (.254)***	1.627 (.355)***
Model Chi-Square	95.72***	49.956***
−2 Log Likelihood	2197.449	1200.308
DF	8	8
Pseudo R-Square (Cox and Snell)	.079	.068
N	1167	705

NOTE: The model uses logistic ordinal regression. Each cell contains the unstandardized coefficients, with standard errors (in parentheses) and level of statistical significance. ***p<.001; **p<.01; *p<.05.

TABLE 6.7 Explaining Pride in Political System

	TIME 1	TIME 2
Gender of Respondent	.020 (.108)	.392 (.120)***
Pay Attention to News	.034 (.007)***	.021 (.008)**
Political Ideology	−.223 (.019)***	−.209 (.022)***
Education	.000 (.004)	−.004 (.004)
Income	−.002 (.002)	−.001 (.002)
Age	.165 (.056)**	.214 (.064)***
Married	.041 (.044)	−.020 (.051)
Religious Attendance	.007 (.008)	.005 (.010)
Constant	5.070 (.213)***	5.475 (.237)***
R-Square	.137	.157
N	1172	704

NOTE: The model uses OLS regression. Each cell contains the unstandardized coefficients, with standard errors (in parentheses) and level of statistical significance. ***p<.001; **p<.01; *p<.05.

CHAPTER 7 | Seeing Women, Strengthening Democracy

IN 1996, WHEN debating the adoption of a gender quota in Mexico, Deputy María Lucero Saldaña Pérez emphasized that "women express themselves with a different voice" (Chamber 10/17/1996). Deputy Adriana Luna Parra argued for the quota by explaining that the country needed a "feminine point of view" and that legislative decision making required "a gendered perspective" (Chamber 11/14/1996). Nearly two decades later, as Chile debated its own affirmative action measure to increase women's representation, Deputy Clemira Pacheco stated: "If we manage to increase (female representation) this means a different outlook" (*Cooperativa* 1/22/2015). And in 2018, as an Argentine province debated parity legislation, provincial deputy Silvia Rojas stated: "this law will guarantee that we can sit in those places because it's us, it's us women who are the ones who raise the issues and the problems that concern us" (*Misiones Online* 5/30/2018).

For more than a quarter century, debates like these have been raging as countries throughout the world consider policies to increase women's presence in politics. These deliberations repeatedly stress that augmenting women's numbers will transform policy. Proponents of these types of affirmative action measures pushed for their adoption because women will introduce a different perspective and focus on different issues.

And yet, as we have demonstrated throughout this book, increasing the number of women in office does *more* than just change policy and the policy process; it alters how female citizens engage with the political process and connect to their governments. When women see women represented in their country's most important political bodies, it sends

Seeing Women, Strengthening Democracy. Magda Hinojosa and Miki Caul Kittilson, Oxford University Press (2020).
© Oxford University Press. DOI: 10.1093/oso/9780197526941.001.0001.

important messages about how the country treats them as citizens. When the message coming through is no longer "politics is a man's game," the ties that link female citizens to the democratic process strengthen. Women become more engaged (they watch the game, follow the players, and know the stats) and more supportive (they have confidence in the referees and value the integrity of the game).

Seeing women strengthens democracy. Greater political interest, knowledge, confidence in understanding politics, and trust in elections and institutions allows women to realize their potential as full democratic citizens. And the implications extend to the collective good as well. Gender differences in positive sentiments toward the political system and its institutions may shape gender differences in the way policy preferences are formed and constructed, and the means by which men and women bring their preferences to their representatives. The historic gendered division of labor in society and women's lived experiences mean that women bring different backgrounds and perspectives to politics. Certainly women are not a monolithic group, and the inclusion of all women is needed for a robust democracy. The absence of full engagement by women limits the richness of the political agenda and the contours of collective deliberation.

In Chapter 1, we documented gender differences in political engagement across 18 countries in Latin America, and in Chapter 3 we noted the variation across countries and over time within a few select cases that had seen sizable increases in women's political presence. We argue that gender differences in connections to the democratic process are not rooted in any deficiencies to be overcome by women, but rather in the exclusionary signals sent by the political arena. The historic exclusion of women from elected office and their persistent underrepresentation serve as symbols about who should and should not be interested in, attentive to, and confident in their assessments about politics.

We have intentionally covered a comprehensive array of political predispositions, attitudes, and orientations. Analyzing each of them separately offered the potential of finding stronger effects for particular attitudes over others. Instead, what we found are coherent patterns. Linking these pieces together, then, what we uncover is a wholesale change in women's connections to democracy. In the case of Uruguay, in Chapters 5 and 6 we find robust patterns across multiple measures of political engagement and political support. Gender differences in political interest, political knowledge, and sense of internal efficacy that were statistically significant before the momentous election fade away after the election. And closing the gap is largely due to women's higher political engagement. The one exception among indicators of engagement is political discussion. Because discussion is an activity, it is possible that other factors work to encourage or discourage political discussion, including involvement in social groups, which is outside the scope of our study.

Women and men start on nearly equal footing before the election in their trust in elections, the legislature, and other political institutions, and in their satisfaction with and pride in the democratic system. After the election, women report higher levels of trust and satisfaction, and the gender differences become statistically significant. Simply put, we find that in the case of the 2014 Uruguayan election, women's inclusion among elected representatives fosters a sense of belonging and commitment to the democratic process among female citizens.

Our findings improve our understanding of comparative political behavior. A voluminous and impactful body of literature examines how publics think and feel about politics, and how these sentiments contribute to the legitimacy and stability of democratic regimes (Almond and Verba 1963; Inglehart 1977; Booth and Seligson 1984; Kaase and Newton 1995; Mishler and Rose 1996; Seligson 2002). Many of these studies consider contextual influences, including regime change and generational structure. However, the bulk of this research overlooks the differential effects for men and for women. Often multivariate analyses will control for gender, but gender is infrequently the focus of the study. In a political context in which there are groups that are largely excluded from the elite level, it is unlikely that influences on political attitudes work the same way for both political insiders and outsiders. Based on the gender differences we have uncovered and the way elite-level representation concentrates its effects on female citizens, future studies in the field of comparative political behavior should more carefully theorize and account for gender differences.

Will the effects we find for gender differences in engagement and support carry to political activities? Theories of symbolic representation have forecast that the effects of symbols will be found in attitudes and orientations (Pitkin 1967). Any effects on political participation would flow through attitudinal changes first, and this psychological connection then would be expected to spur political activity. Because the propensity to participate in politics also rests on opportunities, mobilization, and individual resources, the direct effects of symbols may be more difficult to observe. Future research should attempt to assess the impact of these symbols on political activity.

Visible Gains, Observable Implications

Including significant numbers of women in politics strengthens the connection between female citizens and the political system and its institutions, but only when such changes in women's representation are visible. The previous chapters have empirically demonstrated that stubborn gender gaps can be overcome. Visible gains in the political presence of women boost women's political interest, knowledge, and perceived understanding of important political issues.

Political support, we show, is also gendered. Improvements in women's descriptive representation have follow-on effects not only for political engagement but also for political support. When female citizens see a big jump in women in politics, they express more trust in political institutions and government, becoming more politically supportive than their male counterparts.

While our robust findings from the Uruguayan case demonstrate that when women make visible gains in the political arena, women's political engagement and political support rises, past research has found mixed effects. We argue that, in part, this is because women's inclusion among political elites is not always visible. As our unique Uruguayan survey data show, the assumption of widespread knowledge of gender quotas is misguided. Building our visible cue theory of representation, we argue that visibility of either a policy change—like the adoption of quota legislation—or an increase in women's descriptive representation is vital and cannot be taken for granted. Discerning whether the public has become aware of these changes requires investigation; assessing the visibility of these types of changes requires in-depth knowledge of a case.

Moreover, detecting the effects of quotas and descriptive representation can be complicated, and not just because these changes in the status quo are not always visible. A variety of factors influence citizens' political engagement and support. Numerous symbols and events contend for the public's attention—from widespread images and slogans, to new policies, to scandals and changes in government. Even if the changes that we are interested in are visible, there may be more salient political changes afoot. Women's inclusion at the elite level is just one factor among many affecting individuals' orientations toward their political world.

Further, assessing changes to political engagement and political support as a result of women's increased descriptive representation requires precise methods. As noted in Chapter 3, publicly available survey data, such as the LAPOP or the World Values Survey, may be inadequate for testing the kinds of questions that we pose in this book. Unlike our Uruguayan survey, those surveys are not timed to ideally assess how citizens' attitudes might change as a result of the election of a sizable number of women to office. Neither are those surveys timed to avoid conflating the effects of descriptive representation from the possible effects of changes to substantive representation; in other words, those surveys are not scheduled for the time period after elections but before a new congress is seated.

Notwithstanding the complexities of engaging citizens in the democratic process, we demonstrate that more inclusive decision-making bodies can exert some influence. Policymakers should take notice: while the passage of gender quotas may not have an effect on citizens, the resultant gains in the number of women in political office do have consequences for political engagement and political support. While policymakers discuss the effects that increased women's representation will have on the substantive representation of half the electorate, they routinely overlook the effects that such visible descriptive representation will have for the connections between citizens and democracy.

In addition to discussing the implications of our findings for policy, this chapter explores the potential for the effects of sizable, visible jumps in women's descriptive representation to decay over time. After comparing Uruguayan men's and women's political engagement and support in 2019, we introduce the possibility that the changes that we identified in Chapters 5 and 6 may be short-term effects. We also discuss how failure, skepticism, and novelty may play a role in eroding political connections, and conclude by offering ideas for creating long-lasting change.

Decaying Effects of Including Women

We have documented how a visible change in representatives—how the changing face of representation in Uruguay—had demonstrable effects on ordinary female citizens. Women became more politically connected as a result of rising levels of descriptive representation. But, would these changes last? Would a one-time jump in women's representation in positions of power have enduring effects on how women connect to their government and the political system?

To answer this question, we analyzed the most recent wave of LAPOP which queried 1,581 Uruguayans between March 8 and May 19, 2019. This survey, then, comes more than four years after the second wave of our panel survey, almost four and a half years after the 2014 elections. As described in Chapters 5 and 6, immediately after the 2014 election our panel survey found that gender gaps in political engagement had evaporated and that women displayed more political support than men. Figure 7.1 displays average levels of political interest and satisfaction with democracy, for men and for women, in 2019.

The data paint a somber picture: just a few short years after Uruguayan women closed the gender gap—becoming as politically connected as their male counterparts—gender differences return. By 2019, Uruguay looks much as it had years earlier. Statistically significant differences exist for both political interest and democratic satisfaction, with men once again more interested in politics and now also more satisfied with democracy than women. Importantly, there had not been a national election since our 2014 election of interest (the national election was held months after the LAPOP survey in late October 2019). Thus, reverting to the traditional gender gaps is not the result of a newly elected parliament or a change in governmental direction, but must rest with other factors.

Why have women's gains in political engagement and support eroded? Our visible cue theory of representation emphasizes the dynamic nature of

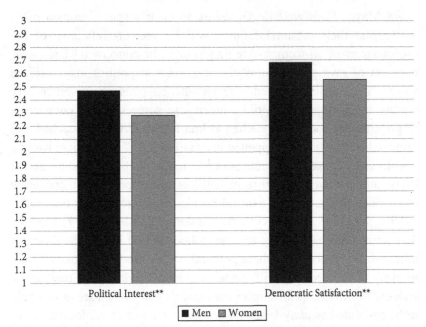

FIGURE 7.1 Political Interest and Satisfaction with Democracy in 2019

NOTE: For political interest and democratic satisfaction, means are presented for each group based on a four-category scale from lowest to highest. ***p<.001; **p<.01; *p<.05.

SOURCE: LAPOP 2019.

representation. We cannot assume that the effects of changes in descriptive representation will always be positive. In the sections to follow we offer scenarios that could lead to the erosion of political connections. Each of these may undermine political connections, making them important for future study. First, we discuss the role of failure, as well as the ways that women may be set up for failure. Second, we explore the role of skepticism in setting the stage for declining political connections. Finally, we consider the ephemeral nature of novelty effects.

When Women Fail . . .

> First of all, I was concerned not to let down all those people who
> had placed their faith in me; but I also felt that if I were to fail,
> people would not see this merely as a personal failure on my part,
> but would say instead that women were not up to the task. Many
> people wondered about that: whether a woman would be able to be an
> effective mayor.

—Ana Luisa Rodríguez de González, Mayor of Atiquizaya, El Salvador (UNDP, N.D.)

As Mayor Rodríguez de González so clearly states, women often worry that their personal failures will be seen as reflective of the inadequacies of all women. Are they right to be concerned? The incorporation of ever greater numbers of women in politics may increase women's political connectedness, but what happens when women very visibly fail? For example, did women lose some sense of connection to government and politics when Dilma Rousseff was impeached and removed from office, as happened in Brazil in 2015? What might happen if voters elect a parity Senate, as in Mexico in 2018, but women do not bring radical change? Do citizens still feel that empowerment and sense of connection that women's initial visible foray into politics brought?

The glass cliff theory (Ryan and Haslam 2007; Funk 2017) suggests that women are more likely to enter politics during precarious times. In other words, in contexts where political parties are faring poorly or are unlikely to succeed they will choose women as leaders or as candidates. Evidence from European democracies reveals that women are more likely to be appointed as party leaders when the party's electoral fortunes have waned (O'Brien 2015). A paradigmatic example of this might be the selection of Theresa May as Prime Minister of Great Britain at a time of upheaval due to the Brexit negotiations.

The reasons that parties might choose women during rocky circumstances include (1) considering women to be sacrificial lambs that are dispensable; (2) leaving choice posts for men and granting women access to less attractive positions; (3) providing women with these positions as a way to let them "prove themselves"; and (4) signaling a change in course by choosing an "outsider" in order to improve the situation (Funk 2017: 16). Similarly, Funk, Hinojosa, and Piscopo 2019 argue that when voters are especially concerned with corruption or their levels of political distrust have risen, parties are more likely to choose female candidates due to stereotypes about women as more honest.

With growing numbers of women in office, we are destined to see women make mistakes. But additionally, we may want to consider the role of often unrealistic expectations that women face. Female politicians may be hampered by expectations that they transform or "clean up" politics overnight. If even one woman does not live up to expectations, public perceptions of that elected official (or even all women in politics) may turn negative. Consequently, female citizens may lose political interest, disengage from the political arena, and return to previous levels of trust and satisfaction with government. In other words, the changes that we see in political connectedness may be a reflection of citizens' oversized expectations of women politicians. Failure, then, may be relative.

These expectations of women politicians may be specifically tied to their supposed gender loyalties: women may perceive that the increase in female descriptive representation did not come with concomitant change in the substantive representation of women in Uruguay. Long-term studies capable of assessing citizens' familiarity with substantive changes of representation may be able to tease out these effects.

Women may also be seen to fail given the "double binds" that they face as they take on their new political roles (Murray 2010). In carrying out these duties, female politicians may be penalized for being too masculine or too feminine, for being too young or too old, for having too little experience or too much (and therefore not signifying "change"). As former Brazilian President Dilma Rousseff explained, "They accused me of being overly tough and harsh, while a man would have been considered firm, strong. Or they would say I was too emotional and fragile, when a man would have been considered sensitive. I was seen as someone too obsessed with work, while a man would have been considered hard-working" (Londoño 2017: np). Given these constraints, women in politics may be continuously fighting perceptions that they are failing. Female citizens may then pick up on two separate cues that might affect their political engagement and support: (1) that women in politics are doing a poor job; or (2) that women in politics have the deck stacked against them.

Our Uruguayan data cannot capture whether real or perceived failures by the new female members of parliament led to decays in women's political connections. But future research should endeavor to empirically assess how failure (real, perceived, or created) can undermine gains in women's political connections.

Visible Cues, Skeptical (and even Antagonistic) Citizens

Citizens may also view the inclusion of women into politics skeptically, changing the nature of the cue and producing disaffected citizens. Women's political inclusion may not always be perceived as part of a holistic change. For example, the election of a woman president or appointment of a few women to a presidential cabinet may not signal women's inclusion in politics as normal or routine, but may instead be interpreted as a one-off event or as pure tokenism, sending a different signal from wholesale inclusion of women into politics.

Similarly, the adoption of gender quotas may not signal larger structural or cultural changes. For example, the move to gender parity legislation in Panama was greeted with skepticism because the country had long had an ineffective gender quota. Eyra Ruíz, head of the women's wing of the *Partido Revolucionario Democrático* stated: "These black and white letters on paper don't do anything. The articles of that law, just like the current one . . . do not impose any type of penalty against parties that fail to comply" (Gray 2015: 299). Quotas and other affirmative action measures—especially those that are seen as feeble—may change the nature of the cue. As Zetterberg explains, women might doubt their government's "true commitment to gender equality" (Zetterberg 2009: 725).

Rather than interpreting the incorporation of women into politics as indicative of a more inclusive political system that values women, skeptical citizens may instead perceive that male and female politicians are not being treated equally. A former Honduran deputy explained that "Congress is a difficult place, not just because of our relations with male deputies, but also with the media . . . You have to put up with all sorts of teasing, nicknames, criticism about what you wear, harassment, and even physical violence" (Ferreira Rubio 2013: 16). If citizens see that women in politics are not being treated like their male colleagues, this too changes the cue.

If women are seen in politics but not yet heard (Morgan and Hinojosa 2018), the public may have doubts about the work that such women do. Recent work finds that while gender-equitable membership on committees confers legitimacy, including just one woman member provides no such rewards, indicating that "citizens cannot be swayed by the presence of a token group representative" (Clayton, O'Brien, and Piscopo 2019: 127).

In addition to skepticism, women's greater political inclusion may butt up against more antagonistic sentiments. As we discussed in Chapter 2, there may be reason to fear backlash. Quotas may lead to increased resentment among men (Franceschet, Krook, and Piscopo 2012; Clayton 2015). Increases in women's descriptive representation may not sit well with some, and could potentially lead to declining political connections for men, who may feel displaced.

The data from Uruguay indicate that the initial change in women's descriptive representation was not viewed with skepticism. Shortly after the election, women were more politically engaged than before, and previously recorded gender gaps had largely been closed. Women also expressed greater levels of political support then men, reversing previous patterns. The decline in women's political engagement and support to pre-2014 levels may mark newfound skepticism or the emergence of animus.

Is This Just A Novelty Effect?

Another possible explanation for the apparent short-term effects of big jumps in women's numbers in office is that the initial surge in women's representation produced a novelty effect—and novelty effects, by definition, will prove short-lived. Novelty is usually tied to the "first woman" frame, as when a woman is elected for the first time to the presidency or to a gubernatorial post (Murray 2010). Beckwith refers to this phenomenon in freshly elected legislatures as "newness," noting that it is "characterized by a range of uncertainties and unpredictabilities" (2007: 43). The concepts of novelty and newness inherently come with an expiration date, since the novelty will inevitably wear off. But, can the effects that we found be simply a reflection of novelty? Could the novelty have worn off within a few years?

Beauregard points out that the "findings on the influence of women's representation occur under specific circumstances—that is, when they are cued by electoral campaigns or candidates. When the impact of women's representation is analyzed over a longer period of time, little effect is found on gender gaps in political engagement or political participation" (Beauregard 2018: 240). It may be that female citizens are cued during the campaign stage—that the campaign itself lends novelty—and that once the campaign is over and women take office, these effects disappear. This would be in keeping with work by Reingold and Harrell 2010, which finds that women are more politically engaged when they have the option to vote for female candidates, but having a female officeholder does not affect their political engagement.

Few studies have directly addressed novelty effects (but see, for example, Murray 2010; Gilardi 2015; Kerevel and Atkeson 2015; Schwindt-Bayer and Reyes-Housholder 2017), but those studies that have examined novelty effects have not assessed how long such effects may last; like Schwindt-Bayer and Reyes-Housholder 2017, we believe that the durability of novelty effects is important for future studies. We expect that novelty effects may diminish based on the strength of the original cue: the novelty of a female governor may dull faster than the novelty of a female president. In an analogous manner, we expect that the novelty of seeing women obtain 20 percent representation in the legislature will vanish more quickly than 40 percent representation would.

Our Uruguayan results then may have captured a shift in time. The 2014 elections and the subsequent announcement of women's historic gains led to women's increased political engagement and support. Nearly five years later, female citizens may have become accustomed to new levels of women's descriptive representation. Political engagement and support may have waned as the novelty of having women in office wore off.

Building Sustainable Change

What can be done to close these gender gaps in political engagement for good? What sorts of structures and policies foster enduring connections between female citizens and their governments? First, we suggest that boosting women's descriptive representation might permanently alter citizens' connections to politics by signaling to women that they are finally full and equal citizens. Relatedly, we argue that gender parity—because of its messaging about the proper role of women in politics—can introduce longer-lasting effects. Second, we propose that intensifying the visibility of women's descriptive representation—and of efforts by the government to fully integrate women into politics—can have durable results. Finally, we suggest that ultimately women must perceive that politics is not just diverse but genuinely inclusive, in order for these gains to last.

What if women's share of legislative seats surged to 45 percent or 55 percent? Might this change the way female citizens, in particular, are politically connected? Scholars have long been interested in how the effects of women's representation respond to incrementally larger proportions of women in office (see, for example, Kanter 1977 and Beckwith 2007). More recently, others have asked: "does the threshold of 30 percent, often considered a critical mass of group representation, generate the same legitimacy beliefs as parity?" (Clayton, O'Brien, and Piscopo 2019: 127).

We argue that as women's share of parliamentary seats becomes more equitable, as women's political presence becomes as visible as men's, female citizens will become more politically engaged and supportive. The message that women are full and equal citizens matters. The message however must be seen, which is why we focus on big jumps in Chapter 3 of this book and then examine in detail the case of Uruguay, where women's numbers in the Senate doubled.

Comparative research demonstrates that gender quotas, when properly designed, can bring meaningful change in women's descriptive representation (Htun and Jones 2002; Tripp and Kang 2008; Krook 2010; Franceschet, Krook, and Piscopo 2012). So although our work shows that gender quotas may not directly impact the public's engagement with or support for politics due to low visibility, these quotas can indirectly improve citizen connections with the democratic process. Sizable gains in women's election exert effects for democratic connections, and these effects are stronger for women.

But additionally, we believe that the decay in women's political connections captured by the 2019 survey data indicates that even big jumps in women's parliamentary representation are not equal to seeing women occupy half the seats and hold half the power. Female citizens may not be placated for long with a bit more of the political pie in the form of a 30 percent quota. Only true equity will change the cue.

A possible reason for the decay in women's political connections may stem from having seen a surge in women's political presence: after women gain political power, female citizens may want more. Rather than appease women, obtaining greater political representation may whet their desire for something more: equality. They may no longer be satisfied with occupying about a third of seats in the Senate and only about one in five seats in the Chamber of Representatives. The effects that we see in 2019 may be indicative of women's sense that these higher levels of women's descriptive representation remain inadequate. Given that women comprise half the population, they may be dissatisfied with anything less than equitable representation in their nation's political posts.

We therefore ask: would parity send a different message? More and more countries have opted to pursue parity—requiring gender-balanced representation in their legislative bodies—rather than mandating that a set percentage of candidates be women. The passage of gender parity legislation may send a different message than a gender quota can. As Lombardo and Meier explain: "A 50-50 percent gender quota or an equal number of men and women stands for a conviction that both sexes are and/or should be equal . . . turning the concept of equality into a political goal that is put centre stage" (Lombardo and Meier 2014: 129–130). As an Uruguayan deputy explained, "Parity is one thing and another thing is for them to give you a percentage . . . conceptually, it's different" (Interview, June 20, 2015).

While many see parity as a 50 percent quota, parity proponents have instead argued that parity is not a short-term affirmative action measure, but rather a permanent expression of equality between citizens. As Piscopo explains: "parity proponents largely argue that gender balance—rather than a minimum percentage of women—constitutes the most legitimate configuration of the democratic state" (2016: 214). These proponents of parity further argue that "parity expresses (rather than just advances) democracy" (Piscopo 2016: 226). Parity may therefore change the messaging that citizens receive. Rather than send the message that gender quotas are needed due to women's historic underrepresentation, parity may instead signal that both men and women are full and equal citizens. Democracy depends on the equitable incorporation of men and women.

Our findings suggest that long-standing and far-reaching gender gaps in political engagement can be overcome by visible and sizable hikes in women's presence in our political institutions, but incremental increases in the proportion of women in office are less likely to lead to much change. The desire to augment women's political engagement must begin with a commitment to increasing their representation in the institutions of power. Gender parity legislation has the potential to dramatically alter the face of representation.

Efforts to raise the visibility of women in politics—especially when women's inroads into the political sphere are relatively new—may prove effective in building and maintaining political connections. Scholarship in political science has routinely documented that citizens are less knowledgeable about politics than we might expect. This means too that citizens will be unfamiliar with the gender makeup of their representative bodies or even know the name of their mayor or governor. Yet, we believe that more can be done, both by governments and by everyday citizens, to call attention to greater political inclusivity.

On March 8, 2015, the Uruguayan legislature marked International Women's Day by requesting that male parliamentarians take a temporary leave of absence. If a male legislator's alternate was a man, that *suplente* was also asked to step aside so that a female alternate could step in. As one female deputy stated, "There were so many of us. We took a picture and it was just so impressive the number of women" (Interview, June 2, 2015). This effort to transform the Uruguayan parliament even for just a day was seen as more than just a fantastic photo-op but instead as an indication of a changing Uruguay. The photo was circulated in the media and via social media, calling attention to women in politics. More recently, in anticipation of the 2019 elections, Uruguayan female candidates united under the hashtag *#Candidatas*, disseminating photos of the many women that would be running in the elections. In Panama, a civil society group organized the *Marcha de Tacones* (March of the High Heels) in September 2018. The event, in the words of Juana Herrera, president of the organization, was to "bring visibility to women in politics and to motivate the community to back these women. We have to make ourselves seen in the streets" (Agrana 2018: np). The tools of social media can be harnessed to spotlight women's presence and participation in politics. Similarly, governments, civil society organizations, and ordinary citizens in countries across the globe can do more to show women in politics or document the importance of policies like gender quotas to bring individuals into politics.

Increasing the number of women in office and calling attention to these achievements will change the way female citizens are politically engaged and supportive. But if these efforts to promote diversity do not reflect true inclusion, we may not see lasting gains. If women flood into legislative bodies but are not treated as equal members in those hallowed halls, we do not expect that female citizens will stay politically connected. If women are physically present in politics but their voices are not heard, we cannot expect that women will become more politically supportive. If women are able to obtain important political offices but always receive greater scrutiny both as candidates and as officeholders, we do not believe that women will become more politically engaged. These are acts of exclusion that come with their own political messaging. Female citizens will also pick up on these political cues, undoing the positive effects that come from seeing more women in politics.

Implications for Strengthening Democracy

Headlines about disengaged and distrustful citizens drive our central research question: under what conditions do marginalized groups most effectively connect to the democratic process? Taken together, the findings of this book suggest that including marginalized groups among the highest echelons of power draws group members into politics—when the group's gains are highly visible to the public. And it is likely this effect is reciprocal, with more engagement at the mass level fortifying the advancements of the marginalized group at the elite level. In sum, the desire for enduring political connection must begin with a commitment to increasing the representation of marginalized groups in the institutions of power.

Including previously underrepresented groups signifies a break with the past. In turn, visible cues of inclusion elicit stronger feelings of connection to the political process. For cues to be visible, our comparative evidence from Chapter 3 suggests that sizable gains may not be sufficient. Even big changes in the composition of a legislature may be lost among a slew of economic problems, political scandals, or rival policy changes. What is more, the evidence presented at the beginning of this chapter suggests that without sustaining those positive visible cues, the novelty of hard-fought achievements can wear off, even potentially yielding a backlash against a group's recent gains.

Descriptive representation matters for citizen engagement and support for the democratic process. The quality of democracy depends upon strong connections between representatives and the represented. Confidence in elections and other institutions of democratic governance, and in the process itself, builds the legitimacy upon which the regime rests. Stronger engagement at the mass level among traditionally underrepresented groups will expand the political agenda and the scope of debate surrounding important political issues. Those historically excluded from political power often simultaneously face discrimination and unequal outcomes in the economic and social spheres. Thus, marginalized groups bring lived experiences and perspectives that, without their presence, would not otherwise be part of the political discourse. In this way, inclusion transforms the parameters of politics, encouraging innovative and effective solutions to the most pressing challenges faced by societies today.

WORKS CITED

Álvarez, Carlos Fernando. 2017. Nicaragua destaca en materia de participación política de las mujeres en América Latina. Published online in *El 19*, May 17, 2017. https://www.el19digital.com/articulos/ver/titulo:56508-nicaragua-destaca-en-materia-de-participacion-politica-de-las-mujeres-en-america-latina-.

Acuña de Molina, Dalva. 2018. La mujer panameña en la historia nacional, siglos XVIII–XX. Chiriquí: Sistema Integrado de Divulgación Científica de la Universidad Autónoma de Chiriquí.

Agrana, Fabio. 2018. Mujeres realizan "Marcha de Tacones" en Panamá para demostrar fuerza política. Published online in *Agencia EFE*, September 13, 2018. https://www.efe.com/efe/america/sociedad/mujeres-realizan-marcha-de-tacones-en-panama-para-demostrar-fuerza-politica/20000013-3747875.

Alexander, Amy C. 2012. Change in Women's Descriptive Representation and the Belief in Women's Ability to Govern: A Virtuous Cycle. *Politics & Gender* 8 (4): 437–464.

Alexander, Amy C., and Farida Jalalzai. 2020. Symbolic Empowerment and Female Heads of States and Government: A Global, Multilevel Analysis. *Politics, Groups, and Identities* 8 (1): 24–43.

Almond, Gabriel, and Sidney Verba. 1963. *The Civic Culture: Political Attitudes in Five Western Democracies*. Princeton: Princeton University Press.

Altman, David. 2008. Collegiate Executives and Direct Democracy in Switzerland and Uruguay: Similar Institutions, Opposite Political Goals, Distinct Results. *Swiss Political Science Review* 14 (3): 483–520.

Altman, David, and Daniel Chasquetti. 2005. Re-election and Political Career Paths in the Uruguayan Congress, 1985–99. *The Journal of Legislative Studies* 11 (2): 235–253.

Andersen, Kristi. 1975. Working Women and Political Participation, 1952–1972. *American Journal of Political Science* 19 (3): 439–453.

Anderson, Christopher J., André Blais, Shaun Bowler, Todd Donovan, and Ola Listhaug. 2005. *Losers' Consent: Elections and Democratic Legitimacy*. Oxford: Oxford University Press.

Anderson, Christopher J., and Christine A. Guillory. 1997. Political Institutions and Satisfaction with Democracy: A Cross-National Analysis of Consensus and Majoritarian Systems. *The American Political Science Review* 91 (1): 66–81.

Anderson, Christopher J., and Andrew J. LoTiempo. 2002. Winning, Losing and Political Trust in America. *British Journal of Political Science* 32 (2): 335–351.

Arana, Rubí Esmeralda, and María L. Santacruz Giralt. 2005. Opinión Pública Sobre el Sistma Político del País y la Participación de la Mujer en la Política. *Collección Género* No. 2. San Salvador: FUNDAUNGO.

Araújo, Clara, and Ana Isabel García. 2006. Latin America: The Experience and the Impact of Quotas in Latin America. In *Women, Quotas, and Politics*, ed. D. Dahlerup, 83–111. London: Routledge.

Archenti, Nélida, and Niki Johnson. 2006. Engendering the Legislative Agenda With and Without the Quota. *Sociología* 52: 133–153.

Archenti, Nélida, and María Inés Tula. 2014. Cambios Normativos y Equidad de Género. De Las Cuotas a la Paridad en América Latina: Los Casos de Bolivia y Ecuador. *América Latina Hoy* 66: 47–68.

Atkeson, Lonna Rae. 2003. Not All Cues Are Created Equal: The Conditional Impact of Female Candidates on Political Engagement. *The Journal of Politics* 65 (4): 1040–1061.

Atkeson, Lonna Rae, and Nancy Carrillo. 2007. More is Better: The Influence of Collective Female Descriptive Representation on External Efficacy. *Politics & Gender* 3 (1): 79–101.

Azpuru, Dinorah. 2017. Does Gender Make a Difference? In *The Gender Gap in Latin American Politics in Women, Politics and Democracy in Latin America*, eds. Tomáš Došek, Flavia Freidenberg, Mariana Caminotti, and Betilde Muñoz Pogossian, 109–130. New York: Palgrave Macmillan.

Baldez, Lisa. 2004. Elected Bodies: The Gender Quota Law for Legislative Candidates in Mexico. *Legislative Studies Quarterly* 29 (2): 239–258.

Banaszak, Lee Ann, and Eric Plutzer. 1993. Contextual Determinants of Feminist Attitudes: National and Subnational Influences in Western Europe. *American Political Science Review* 87 (1): 147–157.

Barnes, Tiffany D., and Stephanie M. Burchard. 2013. 'Engendering' Politics: The Impact of Descriptive Representation on Women's Political Engagement in Sub-Saharan Africa. *Comparative Political Studies* 46 (7): 767–790.

Barnes, Tiffany D., and Mark P. Jones. 2018. Women's Representation in the Argentine National and Subnational Governments. In *Women, Representation, and Politics in Latin America*, ed. Leslie Schwindt-Bayer, 121–139. New York: Oxford University Press.

Barnes, Tiffany D., and Michelle Taylor-Robinson. 2018. Women Cabinet Ministers and Empowerment of Women: Are the two Related? In *Measuring Women's Political Empowerment across the Globe: Strategies, Challenges and Future Research*, eds. Amy Alexander, Catherine Bolzendahl, and Farida Jalalzai, 229–255. Basingstoke, UK: Palgrave Macmillan.

Beauregard, Katrine. 2017. Quotas and Gender Gaps in Political Participation among Established Industrial Democracies: Distinguishing Within and Across-Country Effects. *Political Research Quarterly* 70 (3): 657–72.

Beauregard, Katrine. 2018. Women's Representation and Gender Gaps in Political Participation: Do Time and Success Matter in a Cross-national Perspective? *Politics, Groups, and Identities* 6 (2): 237–63.

Beckwith, Karen. 1989. Sneaking Women into Office: Alternative Access to Parliament in France and Italy. *Women & Politics* 9 (3): 1–15.

Beckwith, Karen. 2007. Numbers and Newness: The Descriptive and Substantive Representation of Women. *Canadian Journal of Political Science* 40 (1): 27–49.

Beckwith, Karen, and Kimberly Cowell-Meyers. 2007. Sheer Numbers: Critical Representation Thresholds and Women's Political Representation. *Perspectives on Politics* 5 (3): 553–565.

Blais, André, Alexandre Morin-Chassé, and Shane P. Singh. 2017. Election Outcomes, Legislative Representation, and Satisfaction with Democracy. *Party Politics* 23 (2): 85–95.

Bobo, Lawrence, and Franklin D. Gilliam. 1990. Race, Sociopolitical Participation and Black Empowerment. *American Political Science Review* 84 (2): 377–394.

Booth, John A., and Mitchell A. Seligson. 1984. The Political Culture of Authoritarianism in Mexico: A Reexamination. *Latin American Research Review* 19 (1): 106–124.

Booth, John A., and Mitchell A. Seligson. 2009. *The Legitimacy Puzzle in Latin America.* New York: Cambridge University Press.

Bottinelli, Eduardo. 2008. Las carreras políticas de los senadores en Uruguay:¿ cambios o continuidades ante el triunfo de la izquierda? *Revista de Sociología e Política* 16 (30): 29–43.

Bowler, Shaun, and Todd Donovan. 2002. Democracy, Institutions and Attitudes about Citizen Influence on Government. *British Journal of Political Science* 32 (2): 371–390.

Burnet, Jennie E. 2011. Women Have Found Respect: Gender Quotas, Symbolic Representation and Female Empowerment in Rwanda. *Politics & Gender* 7 (3): 303–334.

Burns, Nancy. 2007. Gender in the Aggregate, Gender in the Individual. *Politics & Gender* 3 (1): 104–124.

Burns, Nancy, Kay Lehman Schlozman, and Sidney Verba. 2001. *The Private Roots of Public Action: Gender, Equality, and Political Participation.* Cambridge: Harvard University Press.

Burrell, Barbara. 1997. The Political Leadership of Women and Public Policymaking. *Policy Studies Journal* 25 (4): 565–568.

Cáceres, Adrián. 2018. Hombres y mujeres somos iguales en derechos y dignidad. Published online in *Última Hora*, October 17, 2018. www.ultimahora.com/hombres-y-mujeres-somos-iguales-derechos-y-dignidad-n2773919.html.

Campbell, David E., and Christina Wolbrecht. 2006. See Jane Run: Women Politicians as Role Models for Adolescents. *The Journal of Politics* 68 (2): 233–247.

Carlin, Ryan, Matthew M. Singer, and Elizabeth J. Zechmeister. 2015. *The Latin American Voter.* Ann Arbor: University of Michigan Press.

Carroll, Susan. 1985. Women as Candidates in American Politics. Bloomington: Indiana University Press.

Carroll, Susan. 1994. The Politics of Difference: Women Public Officials as Agents of Change. *Stanford Law and Policy Review* 5: 11–20.

Catterberg, Gabriela, and Alejandro Moreno. 2005. The Individual Bases of Political Trust: Trends in New and Established Democracies. *International Journal of Public Opinion Research* 18 (1): 31–48.

Caul, Miki. 1999. Women's Representation in Parliament: The Role of Political Parties. *Party Politics* 5 (1): 79–98.

Celis, Karen. 2006. Substantive Representation of Women: The Representation of Women's Interests and the Impact of Descriptive Representation in the Belgian Parliament (1900-1979). *Journal of Women, Politics & Policy* 28 (2): 85–114.

Chávez, Franz. 2010. Bolivia: Unprecedented Gender Parity in Cabinet. Inter Press Service News Agency, January 27, 2010. http://www.ipsnews.net/2010/01/bolivia-unprecedented-gender-parity-in-cabinet/.

Chamber of Deputies of the Congress of the United Mexican States. 1996. Daily Debates. October 17, 1996. http://cronica.diputados.gob.mx/DDebates/56/3er/Ord1/19961017.html.

Chamber of Deputies of the Congress of the United Mexican States. 1996. Daily Debates. November 14, 1996. http://cronica.diputados.gob.mx/DDebates/56/3er/Ord1/19961114.html.

Chávez, Franz. Bolivia: Unprecedented Gender Parity in Cabinet. Published online at Inter Press Service News Agency, January 27, 2010. http://www.ipsnews.net/2010/01/bolivia-unprecedented-gender-parity-in-cabinet/.

Choque Aldana, Marlene. 2013. Paridad y alternancia en Bolivia. Avances y desafíos de la participación de las mujeres en la política. In *La apuesta por la paridad: democratizando el sistema político en América Latina: los casos de Ecuador, Bolivia y Costa Rica*, ed. Beatriz Llanos, 121–178. Lima: International IDEA.

Choque Aldana, Marlene. 2014. Avances en la participación política de las mujeres. Caminos, agendas y nuevas estrategias de las mujeres hacia la paridad en Bolivia. *Revista Derecho Electoral* 17 (1): 333–356.

Christy, Carol A. 1987. *Sex Differences in Political Participation: Processes of Change in Fourteen Nations*. New York: Praeger.

Citrin, Jack, and Stoker, Laura. 2018. Political Trust in a Cynical Age. *Annual Review of Political Science* 21 (1): 49–70.

Clayton, Amanda. 2015. Women's Political Engagement Under Quota-Mandated Female Representation: Evidence from a Randomized Policy Experiment. *Comparative Political Studies* 48 (3): 333–69.

Clayton, Amanda, Diana Z. O'Brien, and Jennifer M. Piscopo. 2019. All Male Panels? Representation and Democratic Legitimacy. *American Journal of Political Science* 63 (1): 113–129.

Clucas, Richard A., and Melody Ellis Valdini. 2015. T*he Character of Democracy: How Institutions Shape Politics*. New York: Oxford University Press.

Coffé, Hilde, and Catherine Bolzendahl. 2010. Same Game, Different Rules? Gender Differences in Political Participation. *Sex Roles* 62 (5–6): 318–333.

Conway, M. Margaret. 2001. Women and Political Participation. *Political Science & Politics* 34 (2): 231–233.

Cooperativa. 2015. Ley de Cuotas: Qué opinan las mujeres. *Cooperativa*, January 24, 2015. https://www.cooperativa.cl/noticias/pais/gobierno/ley-de-cuotas/ley-de-cuotas-que-opinan-las-mujeres/2015-01-22/165941.html.

Dahl, Robert E. 1971. *Polyarchy: Participation and Opposition.* New Haven: Yale University Press.

Dahl, Robert E. 1982. *Dilemmas of Pluralist Democracy.* New Haven: Yale University Press.

Dahlerup, Drude, ed. 2006. *Women, Quotas and Politics..* New York: Routledge.

Dahlerup, Drude, and Lenita Friedenvall. 2005. Quotas as a "Fast Track" to Equal Representation for Women: Why Scandinavia is no Longer the Model. *International Feminist Journal of Politics* 7 (1): 26–48.

Dalton, Russell. 2008. Citizenship Norms and the Expansion of Political Participation. *Political Studies* 56 (1): 76–98.

Dalton, Russell J., and Christopher J. Anderson. 2011. *Citizens, Context and Choice.* New York: Oxford University Press.

Dassonneville, Ruth, and Ian McAllister. 2018. Gender, Political Knowledge and Descriptive Representation: The Impact of Long-Term Socialization. *American Journal of Political Science* 62 (2): 249–65.

Davidson-Schmich, Louise K. 2016. *Gender Quotas and Democratic Participation: Recruiting Candidates for Elective Offices in Germany.* Ann Arbor: University of Michigan Press.

Delisa, Carolina. 2016. Mujeres en la política: paso lento en el poder. *El Observador*, December 8, 2016. https://www.elobservador.com.uy/nota/mujeres-en-la-politica-paso-lento-en-el-poder-2016128500.

Desposato, Scott, and Barbara Norrander. 2009. The Gender Gap in Latin America: Contextual and Individual Influences on Gender and Political Participation. *British Journal of Political Science* 39 (1): 141–162.

Devlin, Claire, and Robert Elgie. 2008. The Effect of Increased Women's Representation in Parliament: The Case of Rwanda. *Parliamentary Affairs* 61 (2): 237–254.

Diagnóstico sobre la participación de las mujeres en la política. 2007. Panamá: Programa de las Naciones Unidas para el Desarrollo.

Dolan, Kathleen. 2006. Symbolic Mobilization? The Impact of Candidate Sex in American Elections. *American Politics Research* 34 (6): 687–704.

Dovi, Suzanne. 2002. Preferable Descriptive Representatives: Will Just Any Woman, Black, or Latino Do? *American Political Science Review* 96 (4): 729–744.

Easton, David. 1965. *A Systems Analysis of Political Life.* Chicago: University of Chicago Press.

Easton, David. 1975. A Re-Assessment of the Concept of Political Support. *British Journal of Political Science* 5 (4): 435–457.

El País. 2015. Renuncia de Bianchi, vía para cambiar ley de cuota. *El País.* No author listed. https://www.elpais.com.uy/informacion/renuncia-bianchi-via-cambiar-ley-cuota.html.

Escobar-Lemmon, Maria, and Michelle M. Taylor-Robinson. 2016. *Women in Presidential Cabinets: Power Players or Abundant Tokens?* New York: Oxford University Press.

Espinal, Rosario, and Shanyang Zhao. 2015. Gender Gaps in Civic and Political Participation in Latin America. *Latin American Politics and Society* 57 (1): 123–38.

Espinosa, Isolda. 2011. Honduras: una aproximación a la situación de las mujeres a través del análisis de los indicadores de género. Santiago: Comisión Eeconómica para América Latina.

Espírito-Santo, Ana, and Tània Verge. 2017. The Elusive Measurement of Symbolic Effects on Citizens' Political Attitudes: Survey Experiments as Alternative Avenues. *Politics, Groups, and Identities* 5 (3): 494–499.

Ewig, Christina. 1999. The Strengths and Limits of the NGO Women's Movement Model: Shaping Nicaragua's Democratic Institutions. *Latin American Research Review* 34 (3): 75–102.

Ewig, Christina. 2018. Forging Women's Substantive Representation: Intersectional Interests, Political Parity, and Pensions in Bolivia. *Politics & Gender* 14 (3): 433–459.

Ferreira Rubio, Delia M. 2013. La Participación Política de las Mujeres en Honduras: El camino del reconocimiento de derechos a la presencia efectiva. Washington, DC: Fundación Internacional Para Sistemas Electorales.

Ferrín, Monica, Marta Fraile, and Gema M. García-Albacete. 2019. Adult Roles and the Gender Gap in Political Knowledge: A Comparative Study. *West European Politics* 42 (7): 1368–1389.

Fitz Patrick, Mariel. 2019. Por primera vez, hay igualdad de género en la integración de las listas. *Infobae*, June 22, 2019. https://www.infobae.com/politica/2019/06/22/cierre-de-listas-habra-igualdad-de-genero-en-la-integracion-de-las-listas/.

Fraile, Marta, and Raul Gómez. 2017a. Why Does Alejandro Know More about Politics than Catalina? Explaining the Latin American Gender Gap in Political Knowledge. *British Journal of Political Science* 47 (1): 91–112.

Fraile, Marta, and Raul Gómez. 2017b. Bridging the Enduring Gender Gap in Political Interest in Europe: The Relevance of Promoting Gender Equality. *European Journal of Political Research* 56 (3): 601–618.

Franceschet, Susan, Mona Lena Krook, and Jennifer M. Piscopo, eds. 2012. *The Impact of Gender Quotas*. New York: Oxford University Press.

Franceschet, Susan, and Jennifer M. Piscopo. 2008. Gender Quotas and Women's Substantive Representation: Lessons from Argentina. *Politics & Gender* 4 (3): 393–425.

Freidenberg, Flavia. 2019. La representación política de las mujeres en Honduras: resistencias partidistas y propuestas de reformas inclusivas en perspectiva comparada. Working Paper. Atlanta: The Carter Center.

Funk, Kendall D. 2017. The Causes and Consequences of Women's Representation in Local Governments. PhD Dissertation, Texas A&M University.

Funk, Kendall D., Magda Hinojosa, and Jennifer M. Piscopo. 2017. Still Left Behind: Gender, Political Parties, and Latin America's Pink Tide. *Social Politics* 24 (4): 399–424.

Funk, Kendall D., Magda Hinojosa, and Jennifer M. Piscopo. 2019. Women to the Rescue: The Gendered Effects of Public Discontent on Legislative Nominations in Latin America. *Party Politics*: https://doi.org/10.1177/1354068819856614.

Garcé, Adolfo. 2015. La cuota de género, otra vez. El Observador. January 28, 2015. https://www.elobservador.com.uy/nota/la-cuota-de-genero-otra-vez-20151289300.

Gay, Claudine. 2002. Spirals of Trust? The Effect of Descriptive Representation on the Relationship Between Citizens and Their Government. *American Journal of Political Science* 46 (4): 717–733.

Gibson, James L., Raymond M. Duch, and Kent L. Tedin. 1992. Democratic Values and the Transformation of the Soviet Union. *The Journal of Politics* 54 (2): 329–371.

Gil, Valeria. 2017. El Parlamento aprueba la ley de cuotas sin límite de tiempo. *El País*, October 14, 2017. https://www.elpais.com.uy/informacion/parlamento-aprueba-ley-cuotas-limite.html.

Gilardi, Fabrizio. 2015. The temporary importance of Role Models for Women's Political Representation. *American Journal of Political Science* 59 (4): 957–970.

Gray, Tricia. 2015. Quota Mechanics in Panamá, 1999-2014: 'Se obedece, pero no se cumple'. *Bulletin of Latin American Research* 34 (3): 289–304.

Hansen, Susan B. 1997. Talking about Politics: Gender and Contextual Effects on Political Proselytizing. *The Journal of Politics* 59 (1): 73–103.

High-Pippert, Angela, and John Comer. 1998. Female Empowerment: The Influence of Women Representing Women. *Women and Politics* 19: 53–66.

Hinojosa, Magda. 2012. *Selecting Women, Electing Women: Political Representation and Candidate Selection in Latin America*. Philadelphia: Temple University Press.

Hinojosa, Magda. 2017. An 'Alternate' Story of Formal Rules and Informal Institutions: Quota Laws and Candidate Selection in Latin America. In *Gender and Informal Institutions*, ed. Georgina Waylen, 183–202. Lanham: Rowman and Littlefield.

Hinojosa, Magda, Jill Carle, and Gina Woodall. 2018. Speaking as a Woman: Descriptive Presentation and Representation in Costa Rica's Legislative Assembly. *Journal of Women, Politics & Policy* 59 (4): 407–429.

Hinojosa, Magda, Kim L. Fridkin, and Miki Caul Kittilson. 2017. The Impact of Descriptive Representation on Persistent Gender Gaps: A Natural Experiment in Uruguay. *Politics, Groups, and Identities* 5 (3): 435–453.

Hinojosa, Magda, and Ana Vijil Gurdián. 2012. Alternate Paths to Power? Women's Political Representation in Nicaragua. *Latin American Politics and Society* 54 (4): 61–88.

Hinojosa, Magda, and Jennifer Piscopo. 2013. Promoting Women's Right to Be Elected: Twenty-Five Years of Quotas in Latin America. In *Cuotas de género: visión comparada*, ed. J. A. Luna Ramos, 55–107. Mexico City: Electoral Tribunal of the Federal Judicial Power of Mexico.

Htun, Mala N., and Mark P. Jones. 2002. Engendering the Right to Participate in Decision-Making: Electoral Quotas and Women's Leadership in Latin America. In *Gender and the Politics of Rights and Democracy in Latin America*, eds. N. Craske and M. Molyneux, 32–56. London: Palgrave Macmillan.

Htun, Mala, and Jennifer Piscopo. 2014. Women in Politics and Policy in Latin America and the Caribbean. Conflict Prevention and Peace Forum. CPPF Working Papers on Women in Politics: no. 2. Available at: http://webarchive.ssrc.org/workingpapers/CPPF_WomenInPolitics_02_Htun_Piscopo.pdf.

Inglehart, Ronald. 1977. Political Dissatisfaction and Mass Support for Social Change in Advanced Industrial Society. *Comparative Political Studies* 10 (3): 455–472.

Inglehart, Ronald, and Pippa Norris. 2003. *Rising Tide: Gender Equality and Cultural Change Around the World*. Cambridge: Cambridge University Press.

Instituto Brasileiro de Opinião Pública e Estatística (IBOPE). 2009. Mulheres na Política. https://agenciapatriciagalvao.org.br/mulheres-de-olho/politica/dados-e-pesquisas-politica/pesquisa-ibope-ipg-2009/.

Instituto Nacional de la Mujer (INAMU). 2017. Situación de la Mujer en Panamá, 2014-2016. VII Informe Nacional. Panamá: Gobierno de la República de Panamá.

Inter-Parliamentary Union (IPU). 2019. Statistical Archive: Women in National Parliaments. Accessed March 1, 2019: http://archive.ipu.org/wmn-e/classif-arc.htm.

Jalalzai, Farida. 2015. *Women Presidents of Latin America: Beyond Family Ties?* New York: Routledge.

Johnson, Iryna. 2005. Political Trust in Societies Under Transformation: A Comparative Analysis of Poland and Ukraine. *International Journal of Sociology* 35 (2): 63–84.

Johnson, Niki, ed. 2015. *Renovación, paridad: horizontes aún lejanos para la representación política de las mujeres en las elecciones uruguayas 2014.* Montevideo: Cotidiano Mujer.

Johnson, Niki. 2016. Keeping Men In, Shutting Women Out: Gender Biases in Candidate Selection Processes in Uruguay. *Government and Opposition* 51 (3): 393–415.

Johnson, Niki. 2018. Marginalization of Women and Male Privilege in Political Representation in Uruguay. In *Gender and Representation in Latin America*, ed. L. Schwindt-Bayer, 175–195. New York: Oxford University Press.

Johnson, Niki, and Alejandra Moreni. 2009. Representación política de las mujeres y la cuota en Uruguay. In *Primer Encuentro Nacional de Mujeres Convencionales*. Montevideo, Uruguay. Accessed June 2010: http://www.parlamento.gub.uy/externos/parlamenta/.

Jones, Mark P. 1996. Increasing Women's Representation via Gender Quotas: The Argentine Ley de Cupos. *Women & Politics* 16 (4): 75–98.

Jones, Mark P. 2004. Quota Legislation and the Election of Women: Learning from the Costa Rican Experience. *The Journal of Politics* 66 (4):1203–1223.

Kaase, Max, and Kenneth Newton. 1995. *Beliefs in Government*. New York: Oxford University Press.

Kampwirth, Karen. 2010. Populism and the Feminist Challenge in Nicaragua: The Return of Daniel Ortega. In *Gender and Populism in Latin America: Passionate Politics*, ed. Karen Kampwirth, 162–179. University Park: Pennsylvania State University Press.

Kanter, Rosabeth Moss. 1977. Some Effects of Proportions on Group Life: Skewed Sex Ratios and Responses to Token Women. *American Journal of Sociology* 82 (5): 965–990.

Karp, Jeffrey A., and Susan A. Banducci. 2008. When Politics Is Not Just a Man's Game: Women's Representation and Political Engagement. *Electoral Studies* 27 (1): 105–115.

Kerevel, Yann P., and Lonna Rae Atkeson. Reducing Stereotypes of Female Political Leaders in Mexico. *Political Research Quarterly* 68 (4): 732–744.

Kittilson, Miki Caul. 2005. In Support of Gender Quotas: Setting New Standards, Bringing Visible Gains. *Politics & Gender* 1 (4): 638–645.

Kittilson, Miki Caul. 2016. *Gender and Political Behavior. Oxford Research Encyclopedia of Politics*. Oxford: Oxford University Press.

Kittilson, Miki Caul. 2018. Gender and Electoral Behavior. In *The Palgrave Handbook of Women's Political Rights*, eds. S. Franceschet, M. Krook, and N. Tan, 21–32. London: Palgrave Macmillan

Kittilson, Miki Caul, and Leslie Schwindt-Bayer. 2010. Engaging Citizens: The Role of Power-Sharing Institutions. *The Journal of Politics* 72 (4): 990–1002.

Kittilson, Miki Caul, and Leslie Schwindt-Bayer. 2012. *The Gendered Effects of Electoral Institutions: Political Engagement and Participation*. New York: Oxford University Press.

Klesner, Joseph. 2007. Social Capital and Political Participation in Latin America: Evidence from Argentina, Chile, Mexico and Peru. *Latin American Research Review* 42 (2): 1–32.

Koch, Jeffrey. 1997. Candidate Gender and Women's Psychological Engagement in Politics. *American Politics Research* 25 (1): 118–133.

Konte, Maty, and Stephan Klasen. 2016. Gender Differences in Support for Democracy in Sub-Saharan Africa: Do Social Institutions Matter? *Feminist Economics* 22 (2): 55–86.

Krook, Mona Lena. 2004. Gender Quotas as a Global Phenomenon: Actors and Strategies in Quota Adoption. *European Political Science* 3 (3): 59–65.

Krook, Mona Lena. 2010. *Quotas for Women in Politics: Gender and Candidate Selection Reform Worldwide*. New York: Oxford University Press.

Krook, Mona Lena, and Diana Z. O'Brien. 2010. The Politics of Group Representation: Quotas for Women and Minorities Worldwide. *Comparative Politics* 42 (3): 253–272.

LAPOP. 2019. "The Americas Barometer by the Latin American Public Opinion Project." Available at: https://www.vanderbilt.edu/lapop/.

Lawless, Jennifer L. 2004. Politics of Presence? Congresswomen and Symbolic Representation. *Political Research Quarterly* 57 (1): 81–99.

Levitsky, Steven. 2018. Democratic Survival and Weakness. *Journal of Democracy* 29 (4): 102–113.

Lijphart, Arend. 1997. Unequal Participation: Democracy's Unresolved Dilemma Presidential Address, American Political Science Association, 1996. *American Political Science Review* 91 (1): 1–14.

Lipset, Seymour Martin. 1959. Some Social Requisites of Democracy: Economic Development and Political Legitimacy. *American Political Science Review* 53 (1): 69–105.

Liu, Shan-Jan Sarah. 2018. Are Female Political Leaders Role Models? Lessons from Asia. *Political Research Quarterly* 71 (2): 255–269.

Liu, Shan-Jan Sarah, and Lee Ann Banaszak. 2017. Do Government Positions Held by Women Matter? A Cross-National Examination of Female Ministers' Impacts on Women's Political Participation. *Politics & Gender* 13 (1): 132–62.

Llanos, Mariana, and Francisco Sánchez. 2006. Council of Elders? The Senate and Its Members in the Southern Cone. *Latin American Research Review* 41 (1): 133–152.

Lombardo, Emanuela, and Meier, Petra. 2014. *The Symbolic Representation of Gender: A Discursive Approach*. Farnham: Taylor & Francis Group.

Londoño, Ernesto. 2017. President Bachelet of Chile is the Last Woman Standing in the Americas. *The New York Times*. July 24, 2017. https://www.nytimes.com/2017/07/24/world/americas/michelle-bachelet-president-of-chile.html.

Mansbridge, Jane. 1980. *Beyond Adversary Democracy*. New York: Basic Books.

Mansbridge, Jane. 1999. Should Blacks Represent Blacks and Women Represent Women? A Contingent 'Yes.' *The Journal of Politics* 61 (3): 628–657.

Matland, Richard E., and Michelle M. Taylor. 1997. Electoral System Effects on Women's Representation: Theoretical Arguments and Evidence from Costa Rica. *Comparative Political Studies* 30 (2): 186–210.

Meier, Petra. 2004. The Mutual Contagion Effect of Legal and Party Quotas: A Belgian Perspective. *Party Politics* 10 (5): 583–600.

Millett, Richard L., Jennifer S. Holmes, and Orlando J. Pérez, eds. 2010. *Latin American Democracy: Emerging Reality or Endangered Species?* New York: Routledge.

Mishler, William, and Richard Rose. 1996. Trajectories of Fear and Hope: Support for Democracy in Post-Communist Europe. *Comparative Political Studies* 28 (4): 553–581.

Misiones Online. 2018. Continúa debate legislativo por proyectos de paridad de género. May 30, 2018. https://misionesonline.net/2018/05/30/continua-debate-legislativo-por-proyectos-de-paridad-de-genero/.

Moraes, Juan Andrés. 2008. Why Factions? Candidate Selection and Legislative Politics in Uruguay. In *Pathways to Power: Political Recruitment and Candidate Selection in Latin America*, eds. P. M. Siavelis and S. Morgenstern, 164–86. University Park: Pennsylvania State University Press.

Morgan, Jana, and Melissa Buice. 2013. Latin American Attitudes toward Women in Politics: The Influence of Elite Cues, Female Advancement, and Individual Characteristics. *The American Political Science Review* 107 (4): 644–662.

Morgan, Jana, and Magda Hinojosa. 2018. Women in Political Parties: Seen but not Heard. In *Gender and Representation in Latin America*, ed. L. Schwindt-Bayer, 74–98. New York: Oxford University Press.

Morgenstern, Scott. 2001. Organized Factions and Disorganized Parties: Electoral Incentives in Uruguay. *Party Politics* 7 (2): 235–256.

Murray, Rainbow. 2010. *Cracking the Highest Glass Ceiling: A Global Comparison of Women's Campaigns for Executive Office*. Santa Barbara: Praeger.

Nir, Lilach, and Scott D. McClurg. 2015. How Institutions Affect Gender Gaps in Public Opinion Expression. *Public Opinion Quarterly* 79 (2): 544–67.

Norris, Pippa. 2002. Women's Power at the Ballot Box. In *Voter Turnout Since 1945: A Global Report*, eds. R. Lopez Pintor and M. Gratschew, 98–102. Stockholm: International IDEA.

Norris, Pippa. 2017. The Conceptual Framework of Political Support. In *Handbook on Political Trust*, eds. S. Zmerli and T. van der Meer, 19–32. Northampton: Edward Elgar.

Norris, Pippa, and Mark Franklin. 1997. Social Representation in the European Parliament. *European Journal of Political Research* 32 (2): 185–210.

Oakes, Amy C. 2002. Gender Differences in Support for Democracy. In *Social Structure: Changes and Linkages*, ed. K Slomczynski, 157–173. Warsaw: IFiS.

O'Brien, Diana Z. 2015. Rising to the Top: Gender, Political Performance, and Party Leadership in Parliamentary Democracies. *American Journal of Political Science* 59 (4): 1022–1039.

OEM Editors. 2018. Número de mujeres qué conformarán los Congresos es histórica. *El Sol de México*, July 11, 2018. https://www.elsoldemexico.com.mx/mexico/politica/numero-de-mujeres-que-conformaran-los-congresos-es-historica-1831290.html.

Parra Badilla, Verónica, Miriam Pérez Meneses, and Ronald Sáenz Leandro. 2015. Efectividad de cuotas por razón de género en sistemas de lista alternativos a la bloqueada cerrada: los casos de Panamá y Ecuador. Paper presented at the Congreso Centroamericano de Ciencias Políticas. San José, Costa Rica.

Paxton, Pamela, and Melanie Hughes. 2007. *Women, Politics, and Power: A Global Perspective*. Thousand Oaks: Pine Forge Press.

Pérez, Verónica. 2015. Las mujeres en política en Uruguay. De la cuota a la paridad: una reforma necesaria. Policy Paper N° 5, Santiago: Diego Portales University.

Phillips, Anne. 1995. *The Politics of Presence*. New York: Oxford University Press.

Pintor, Rafael López, and Maria Gratschew, eds. 2002. *Voter Turnout since 1945, A Global Report*. Stockholm: International IDEA.

Piscopo, Jennifer M. 2016. Democracy as Gender Balance: The Shift from Quotas to Parity in Latin America. *Politics, Groups, and Identities* 4 (2): 214–230.

Piscopo, Jennifer M., and Kristin Wylie. Forthcoming. *Gender, Race, and Political Representation*. Oxford: Oxford Research Encyclopedia of Politics.

Pitkin, Hanna F. 1967. *The Concept of Representation*. Berkeley: University of California Press.

PNUD. 2014. Capacitan a mujeres políticas para marcar presencia y ganar liderazgo. September 23, 2014. Available at: http://www.uy.undp.org/content/uruguay/es/home/presscenter/articles/2014/09/23/mujeres-pol-ticas-obtienen-herrmaientas-marcar-presencia-y-ganar-liderazgo.html.

Press Reference. Available at: http://www.pressreference.com/.

Quota Project. 2019. Gender Quotas Database. International IDEA. https://www.idea.int/data-tools/data/gender-quotas.

Reingold, Beth. 2000. *Representing Women: Sex, Gender, and Legislative Behavior in Arizona and California*. Chapel Hill: University of North Carolina Press.

Reingold, Beth, and Jessica Harrell. 2010. The Impact of Descriptive Representation on Women's Political Engagement: Does Party Matter? *Political Research Quarterly* 63 (2): 280–294.

Restrepo Sanín, Juliana. 2016. Violence Against Women in Politics and the Law: Arguments for an Expanded Definition. Paper presented at the World Congress of the International Political Science Association, Poznán, Poland.

Reyes-Housholder, Catherine, and Leslie A. Schwindt-Bayer. 2016. The Impact of Presidentas on Political Activity. In *The Gendered Executive: A Comparative Analysis of Presidents, Prime Ministers, and Chief Executives*, eds. J. Martin and M. Borrelli, 103–122. Philadelphia: Temple University Press.

Reyes-Housholder, Catherine, and Gwynn Thomas. Forthcoming. Gendered Incentives, Party Support and Female Presidential Candidates. *Comparative Politics*.

Rousseau, Stéphanie, and Christina Ewig. 2017. Latin America's Left-Turn and the Political Empowerment of Indigenous Women. *Social Politics* 24 (4): 425–451.

Ryan, Michelle K., and S. Alexander Haslam. 2007. The Glass Cliff: Exploring the Dynamics Surrounding the Appointment of Women to Precarious Leadership Positions. *Academy of Management Review* 32 (2): 549–572.

Saint-Germain, Michelle A., and Cynthia Chávez Metoyer. 2008. *Women Legislators in Central America: Politics, Democracy, and Policy*. Austin: University of Texas Press.

Samqui, Eva. 2016. La paridad en Nicaragua: una ruta impulsada desde la voluntad partidista. In *La democracia paritaria en América Latina: los casos de México y Nicaragua*, ed. B. Llanos, 95–119. Washington, DC: Inter-American Commission of Women.

Sanbonmatsu, Kira. 2003. Gender-Related Political Knowledge and the Descriptive Representation of Women. *Political Behavior* 25 (4): 367–388.

Sanbonmatsu, Kira 2008. Gender Backlash in American Politics? *Politics & Gender* 4 (4): 634–642.

Sánchez Díez, María. 2019. "She's 19 and lives with her mother: Meet the feminist teen-ager running for office in Argentina." *The Washington Post*. October 18, 2019. https://www.washingtonpost.com/world/2019/10/18/shes-lives-with-her-mother-meet-feminist-teenager-running-office-argentina/.

Sapiro, Virginia. 1981. If U.S. Senator Baker Were a Woman: An Experimental Study of Candidate Images. *Political Psychology* 3 (1/2): 61–83.

Sapiro, Virginia, and Pamela Conover. 1997. The Variable Gender Basis of Electoral Politics: Gender and Context in the 1992 US Election. *British Journal of Political Science* 27 (4): 497–523.

Saward, Michael. 2006. The Representative Claim. *Contemporary Political Theory* 5 (3): 297–318.

Saward, Michael. 2010. *The Representative Claim*. New York: Oxford University Press.

Schwindt-Bayer, Leslie. 2006. Still Supermadres? Gender and the Policy Priorities of Latin American Legislators. *American Journal of Political Science* 50 (3): 570–585.

Schwindt-Bayer, Leslie. 2010. *Political Parties and Women's Representation in Latin America*. New York: Oxford University Press.

Schwindt-Bayer, Leslie. 2018. Conclusion: The Gendered Nature of Democratic Representation. In *Gender and Representation in Latin America*, ed. L. Schwindt-Bayer, 245–261. New York: Oxford University Press.

Schwindt-Bayer, Leslie, and Santiago Alles. 2018. Women in Legislatures: Gender, Institutions, and Democracy. In *Gender and Representation in Latin America*, ed. L. Schwindt-Bayer, 56–73. New York: Oxford University Press.

Schwindt-Bayer, Leslie, and William Mishler. 2005. An Integrated Model of Women's Representation. *The Journal of Politics* 67 (2): 407–428.

Schwindt-Bayer, Leslie A., and Catherine Reyes-Housholder. 2017. Citizen Responses to Female Executives: Is It Sex, Novelty or Both? *Politics, Groups, & Identities* 5 (3): 373–398.

Seligson, Mitchell A. 2002. Trouble in Paradise: The Impact of the Erosion of System Support in Costa Rica, 1978-1999. *Latin American Research Review* 37 (1): 160–185.

Sierra, Xiomara Dolores. 2018. La participación y la representación política de las mujeres en Honduras. In *Derechos Políticos de las Mujeres: Avances y Buenas Prácticas en Guatemala y Honduras*, eds. Santa Cruz Sagastume and Wendy Marieth, 185–222. San José, Costa Rica: Instituto Interamericano de Derechos Humanos.

Simien, Evelyn M. 2015. *Historic Firsts: How Symbolic Empowerment Changes U.S. Politics*. New York: Oxford University Press.

Singh, Shane P. 2014. Not all Election Winners are Equal: Satisfaction with Democracy and the Nature of the Vote. *European Journal of Political Research* 53 (2): 308–327.

Solt, Frederick. 2008. Economic Inequality and Democratic Political Engagement. *American Journal of Political Science* 52 (1): 48–60.

Subrayado. 2014. Conozca a las senadoras y diputadas electas el domingo. October 28, 2014. No author listed. https://www.subrayado.com.uy/conozca-las-senadoras-y-diputadas-electas-el-domingo-n38594.

Supreme Electoral Tribunal of Guatemala. 2019. Presidente y Vicepresidente. TSE Guatemala—Elecciones Generales y al Parlamento Centroamericano. https://resultados2019.tse.org.gt/201901/.

Taylor-Robinson, Michelle M. 2009. Honduras: una mezcla de cambio y continuidad. *Revista de Ciencia Política* 29 (2): 471–489.

Taylor-Robinson, Michelle M. 2018. *Gender and Cabinets in Latin America.* Annual Meeting of the American Political Science Association. Boston, MA.

Teledoce. 2014. Debatimos sobre la cuota femenina en la política. Filmed November 6, 2014. https://www.teledoce.com/programas/debatimos-sobre-la-cuota-femenina-en-la-politica/.

Teledoce. 2014. Conozca las nuevas caras del Parlamento. Filmed November 20, 2014. https://www.teledoce.com/ya-emitidos/codigo-pai%C2%ADs/los-parlamentarios-electos-de-cara-al-proximo-periodo-de-gobierno/.

Teledoce. 2015. Graciela Bianchi renunció a su banca como senadora. Filmed January 28, 2015. https://www.teledoce.com/telemundo/nacionales/graciela-bianchi-renuncio-a-su-banca-como-senadora-y-sera-sustituida-por-alvaro-delgado/.

Televisión Nacional Uruguay. 2014. El candidato nacionalista habló de la Ley de Cuotas y del voto en el exterior. Filmed November 21, 2014. https://www.youtube.com/watch?v=kB6QU4PdZLQ.

Televisión Nacional Uruguay. 2015. El nuevo Parlamento. Filmed February 16, 2015. https://www.youtube.com.watch?v=E_zEhVX5zHQ.

Thomas, Sue. 1991. The Impact of Women on State Legislative Policies. *The Journal of Politics* 53 (4): 958–976.

Thove, Karina. 2014. Con la politóloga Niki Johnson: la política del ninguneo hacia las mujeres. *La República*, September 22, 2014. http://www.republica.com.uy/con-la-politologa-niki-johnson-la-politica-del-ninguneo-hacia-las-mujeres/.

Tremblay, Manon, and Réjean Pelletier. 2000. More Feminists or More Women? Descriptive and Substantive Representations of Women in the 1997 Canadian Federal Elections. *International Political Science Review* 21 (4): 381–405.

Tripp, Aili Mari, and Alice Kang. 2008. The Global Impact of Quotas: On the Fast Track to Increased Female Legislative Representation. *Comparative Political Studies* 41 (3): 338–361.

Ulbig, Stacy G. 2007. Gendering Municipal Government: Female Descriptive Representation and Feelings of Political Trust. *Social Science Quarterly* 88 (5): 1106–1123.

UNESCO. 2019. UNESCO Atlas of Gender Inequality in Education. *UIS Tellmaps.* UNESCO. https://tellmaps.com/uis/gender/#!/tellmap/79054752/2.

United Nations, UNDP Annual Report 2007: Making Globalization Work for Everyone. May 10, 2007: https://www.undp.org/content/undp/en/home/librarypage/corporate/undp_in_action_2007.html.

UNDP. Women Gain Ground in El Salvador's Politics. Published online at: http:www.latinamerica.undp.org/content/rblac/en/home/ourwork/democratic-governance/successstories/women-gain-ground-in-el-salvadors-politics.html.

Valdini, Melody E. 2019. *The Inclusion Calculation.* New York: Oxford University Press.

Verba, Sidney, Nancy Burns, and Kay Lehman Schlozman. 1997. Knowing and Caring About Politics: Gender and Citizen Engagement. *The Journal of Politics* 59 (4): 1051–1072.

Verba, Sidney, Kay Lehman Schlozman, and Henry E. Brady. 1995. *Voice and Equality: Civic Voluntarism in American Politics*. Cambridge: Harvard University Press.

Verge, Tània, Ana Espírito-Santo, and Nina Wiesehomeier. 2015. The Symbolic Impact of Women's Representation on Citizens' Political Attitudes: Measuring the Effect Through Survey Experiments. Paper presented at the XII Congreso Español de Ciencia Politica y del la Administracion, Género y Poder.

Verge, Tània, and Raquel Pastor. 2018. Women's Political Firsts and Symbolic Representation. *Journal of Women, Politics & Policy* 39 (1): 26–50.

Vincent, Louise. 2004. Quotas: Changing the Way Things Look without Changing the Way Things Are. *The Journal of Legislative Studies* 10 (1): 71–96.

Waldron-Moore, Pamela. 1999. Eastern Europe at the Crossroads of Democratic Transition: Evaluating Support for Democratic Institutions, Satisfaction with Democratic Government, and Consolidation of Democratic Regimes. *Comparative Political Studies* 32 (1): 32–62.

Walker, Lee Demetrius, and Genevieve Kehoe. 2013. Regime Transition and Attitudes Toward Regime: The Latin American Gender Gap in Support for Democracy. *Comparative Politics* 45 (2): 187–205.

Warren, Mark E. 2002. What Can Democratic Participation Mean Today? *Political Theory* 30 (5): 677–701.

Weldon, S. Laurel. 2002. Beyond Bodies: Institutional Sources of Representation for Women in Democratic Policymaking. *The Journal of Politics* 64 (4): 1153–1174.

Wolbrecht, Christina, and David E. Campbell. 2007. Leading by Example: Female Members of Parliament as Political Role Models. *American Journal of Political Science* 51 (4): 921–939.

Wolbrecht, Christina, and David E. Campbell. 2017. Role Models Revisited: Youth, Novelty, and the Impact of Female Candidates. *Politics, Groups, & Identities* 5 (3): 418–434.

World Press Review. Available at: https://www.worldpress.org/.

Wylie, Kristin. 2018. *Party Institutionalization and Women's Representation in Democratic Brazil*. New York: Cambridge University Press.

Zaller, John, and Stanley Feldman. 1992. A Simple Theory of the Survey Response: Answering Questions versus Revealing Preferences. *American Journal of Political Science* 36 (3): 579–616.

Zetterberg, Pär. 2008. The Downside of Gender Quotas? Institutional Constraints on Women in Mexican State Legislatures. *Parliamentary Affairs* 61 (3): 442–460.

Zetterberg, Pär. 2009. Do Gender Quotas Foster Women's Political Engagement?: Lessons from Latin America. *Political Research Quarterly* 62 (4): 715–730.

INDEX

Tables and figures are indicated by *t* and *f* following the page number

For the benefit of digital users, indexed terms that span two pages (e.g., 52–53) may, on occasion, appear on only one of those pages.

Pacheco, Clemira, 126
Panama
    elections (2004) in, 68
    elections (2009) in, 68
    elections (2014) in, 67–69
    gender differences in the politics of,
        14–17f, 68
    legislative gender quota laws in, 23t,
        57n2, 57t, 67–68, 75, 134
    Marcha de Tacones (2018) in, 139
    political engagement levels and, 69
    political interest levels in, 10f, 14f, 68
    political support levels in, 11f, 11–12,
        17f, 69
    women cabinet members in, 5f, 5, 67
    women judges in, 67
    women legislators in, 6f, 57–58n3,
        57–58, 57t, 67–69
    women presidential candidates
        in, 4t, 12
    women presidents in, 67
    women's suffrage in, 67
Paraguay
    gender differences in the politics of,
        14–17f, 16
    legislative gender quota laws in, 23, 23t
    political interest levels in, 10f, 14f
    political support in, 11f, 11–12, 16, 17f
    women cabinet members in, 5f, 5
    women legislators in, 1–2, 6f, 6, 23
    women presidential candidates in,
        1–2, 4t
parity representation, 5, 137–38
Partido Nacional (Uruguay), 88, 91–92
Partido Popular (Panama), 67–68
Pastor, Raquel, 46
Payssé, Daniela, 71
Pérez, Nielsen, 1
Peru
    gender differences in the politics of,
        14–17f, 14, 15, 16
    legislative gender quota laws in, 23t, 75
    political engagement levels in, 15
    political interest levels in, 10f, 14f, 14
    political support levels in, 11f, 11–12,
        16, 17f

women cabinet members in, 5f
women legislators in, 6f
women presidential candidates in,
    1–2, 4t
Phillips, Anne, 31
Piscopo, Jennifer, 138
Pitkin, Hanna F., 45, 53
Poland, 16, 109
political connection
    age factors and, 96
    descriptive representation and, 12, 20,
        21, 27–28, 29, 31, 34, 45–46, 50, 55,
        128, 129, 131–32, 138–39
    gender differences in, 9, 12–17, 45–46,
        50, 96, 127
    legislative gender quotas and,
        47–48, 137
    political support and, 8, 9, 53
    political trust and, 53
    symbolic representation and, 53, 55
    in Uruguay, 96, 128, 131
political discussions
    age levels and, 105t, 106
    education levels and, 96–97, 105t, 106
    as form of political engagement, 8, 15
    gender differences and, 13, 15, 104–6,
        105f, 105t, 107–8, 127–28
    income levels and, 105t
    Latin American countries in
        comparative context and, 15
    marital status and, 105t, 106
    news consumption and, 97, 105t, 106
    political efficacy and, 95, 96f, 102,
        104–6, 105t
    political ideology and, 105t, 106
    political interest and, 95, 96f,
        104–6, 105t
    religiosity and, 105t, 106
    in Uruguay, 104–6, 105f, 105t,
        107–8, 127–28
political efficacy
    age levels and, 103t, 104, 107
    descriptive representation and, 2–3, 28,
        95, 129
    education levels and, 96–97,
        103t, 104